RAISING

S

a

E

H

Reid

Ferguson-Carol Publishers

Raising Kids With Just A Little Cash

Reid, Lisa.
   Raising kids with just a little cash / Lisa Reid.
   p. cm.
   Includes biographical references and index.
   ISBN 0-9651651-0-8
   1 Finance, Personal. 2. Parenting. I.Title.
HG179.R45 1996   332.024'0431
Library of Congress Catalog Number: 96-96469

Ferguson-Carol Publishers
36 Camino Cielo   Santa Fe, NM 87501
(505) 983-3302

First Edition 9 8 7 6 5 4 3 2

Printed in the United States of America
Printed on recycled paper

For

**my husband, Jim, who has helped me
make so many of my dreams come true,**

and for

**my children, Alyssa and Ivy, who
were the inspiration for this book**

Acknowledgements

I received help from many quarters during book writing and production. Gratitude is owed to everyone whose support, kind words and prayers provided encouragement. Special thanks to the following folks:

Lexie Curtis, Kat Duff, Celeste and Kenny Epstein, Carol Fitzgerald, the staff at Gilliand Printing, Joyceanne Hagberg, Sue Hodgson, Nichoe Lichen, Linda Loux, Helen and Neal Lowe, Celina McClaren, Jill Miyagawa, Neil Miller, Amadea Morningstar, Pat Norris, Linda Prince, Karen Rafferty, Ceu Ratliffe and Landis Smith.

TABLE OF CONTENTS

Normal is getting dressed in clothes that you buy for work, driving through traffic in a car that you are still paying for, in order to get to the job that you need so that you can pay for the clothes, car and the house that you leave empty all day in order to afford to live in it.

Ellen Goodman

INTRODUCTION

Raising a child may be the most costly, tiring, challenging and satisfying thing you ever do. In fact, sometimes the money and personal energy requirements seem simply overwhelming. The USDA estimates that it can cost up to $334,600 to raise your child to age 18! Families in the U.S. spend over fifty billion dollars yearly on their children's food, clothing, entertainments and vacations. With the financial and energy requirements of parenting at such an enormous level, it is no wonder that fatigue is the single biggest thing that brings mothers into doctor's offices.

Take hope! This book is about the money required to get our children from infancy to adulthood and how we can do it for a lot less than is commonly assumed. Families all over are discovering the joy, the ease, the *relief* they feel as they reduce expenses. Throughout the book you'll hear ideas from real families who are raising their kids for less, often on one income.

This book is also about energy - the personal energy that we spend to make our money. Joe **Dominguez** and Vicki Robin, in their excellent book, *Your Money or Your Life,* call this "life energy" - the very essence of our life that we trade when we exchange our time for money, and our money for material goods and services. Do we have to spend all our money, and sometimes more, to raise our kids? Is there another way?

Yes, there is! It's an old concept called thrift. Not deprivation, not boredom, not poverty - thrift. Thrift is being efficient with your life energy and money, spending it in ways that bring you the biggest value. Being thrifty has been one of the most empowering experiences I have ever had, as you'll see when you read the story of my family's transition to a thrifty lifestyle. The act of being thrifty has given me so many more possible life choices and I am still amazed to find that, although we are living on less money, our lives are immeasurably richer.

How to Use This Book

Today it is very common for families to be stretched beyond the limits of their finances, time and energy. If this is true for your family, you can attest that it is anxiety-provoking to live in this situation! This book provides three things that will help you and your family to stop being uncomfortably stretched.

1. **Instructions for specific money-saving actions** you can take in areas every parent encounters: Clothes, Toys, Entertainment and Education, Birthday parties, Food, Health, Travel and Holidays.

2. **Inspiring stories about real families** who have made the transition to thrifty living.

3. A means of evaluation, The Time is Money Saved Formula, to help you decide which actions are most deserving of your time.

More Money Is Not The Only Answer

Many of us live in relative abundance, yet experience an underlying uneasiness. We may unconsciously, or even consciously, realize what the acquisition of material goods at such an extreme level is costing our families. Juliet Schor, in *The Overworked American* says that people are working one month per year more than they used to in 1969. Polls show that although Americans own more of the appliances and material possessions thought to constitute the good life, they feel significantly less well-off than they did twenty years ago.

We have an idea that we "must have" VCR's and $150 Nikes and so we end up with our houses, garages and even storage units stuffed full. We "indulge" our children, we "reward" ourselves. I certainly did all of those things. When my oldest child was a baby, I discovered mall cruising. I thought of it as a nice outing for us. And before she was two, she had a room packed full of goodies and I had a house packed full of stuff. We also had a house mortgage, a mortgage on a piece of land, a mortgage on a timeshare condo, a roof that needed to be replaced and an income that barely stretched to cover everything. Our credit cards were creeping up, up, up, but we always figured out a way to make ends meet. I had faith that we would do whatever it took to pay our bills, and yet I couldn't shake that nagging uneasiness. I was being swept along financially and I wasn't the sweeper, I was the thing being swept!

We had dreams: a better house, a full-time parent at home, a savings account. It became very clear to me that unless things changed, those dreams were probably not going to become reality.

I did one thing that made my spending choices very clear. For one month, I wrote down every single thing on which we spent money. I highly recommend this basic exercise for anyone interested in looking at their spending patterns. What I saw was the shocking amount we spent on what I thought of as "piddly stuff", and on food, especially eating out. I would never have considered making a casual decision about buying something big like a TV, but for what I casually spent day in and day out, I could have almost paid for one!

What an eye-opener! My husband, Jim, and I talked about it for many evenings and came to the agreement that we would take whatever actions required to reduce our expenses and that we would begin to focus on building a house on our land. With a lot of excitement, and some trepidation, we took our children (we had a second one by then - six weeks old), sold our house and moved into a tiny apartment. Many people questioned our judgement, but most were too polite to mention it at the time.

Our apartment didn't have amenities like a dish-washer, a washer or a dryer, but it was within walking distance of many interesting, free activities. We started to replace going out and spending money with just going out to places where we didn't need to spend money. We continued to track our expenditures and look at them more critically - asking if they would really enrich our lives. We had such a tiny space that we were reluctant to buy much for the children. After all, we already had toys and games packed up in our storage unit, as well as kitchen things, linens, furniture, books and quite a few boxes marked "Miscellaneous".

After some months of living with fewer things, we discovered we kind of liked it. It was freeing. One experience reinforced these feelings. I went to a party at a friend's house which was tiny, like mine. Her neighbor entered, carring four glasses, which she was loaning to my friend for the evening. A light bulb went off in my head - my friend had eight glasses only. Eight glasses to move, for which to find cupboard space and to maintain. How easy to find more if she needed them once or twice a year. I had always admired her kitchen. It was almost Zen-like in its order and beauty. Now I was finally grasping the choices my friend had made which let that atmosphere of order emerge.

At home, I looked at our possessions. We had pared down considerably and yet we still had an abundance of food, clothes, toys, books and entertainment. I began to wonder if having a large quantity of stuff really made our lives any better. Besides the money that we spent to get it, just having so many possessions felt like a burden.* As I began to consider this question, we were at the same time planning our new house. I will always be thankful that we had the experience of living successfully in a small space and had begun to look more carefully at our expenditures *before* we built the house. It affected the decisions we were making right then.

We decided to keep the house at under 1500 square feet so that we could put a limit on how much time and money (life energy) we would need to expend in paying for the house. We decided our two girls could share a room and that our family could live with one bathroom. We decided not to buy a lot of new furniture right away and even to put our mattress on the floor until we could find an inexpensive bed frame. We decided to do as much of the work ourselves as possible.

That was Phase I of our self-imposed crash course on learning to live with less. Phase II happened after we moved into our completed house. I had continued to work in my counseling practice during the house-building years although I had shifted the hours to weekends and evenings to minimize the need for babysitters. Jim and I had begun to homeschool our oldest daughter, Alyssa, then seven years old. From our new house it was a longer commute to town and I really didn't like being away in the evening. Plus, Jim and I were both tired all the time!

I *was* a lot happier with the direction our family life was taking, but I wanted more. Like many other moms, I began

---

* Now, after years of simplifying and paring down, I still have this question. Free and low-cost toys and clothes are really so readily available that we end up with lots. Acquiring only what the family will use, whether it is free or not, is a high-level skill that I am still honing.

to try to figure out a way to work from home. I wanted flexible hours, low overhead and work that could be done while I was with the children. After considering and discarding several ideas, I had a brainstorm. The next day I hired myself to be "the family money-saver".

I paid myself with all the money we *didn't spend* because of the actions I took as the "money-saver". While my two-year-old played on the floor next to me, I made a list of all our credit cards and their annual fees. While she napped, I called and cancelled every one that wouldn't waive the fee. For that hour's work, I saved us $60. I would have had to earn at least $75 to take home $60.

After that, I was on a roll. Seeing "money-saver" as my job seemed to make it easier for me to take on cooking, sewing or bargain-hunting that I had previously shunned because they took too much time. By tracking the hours I spent and the money we saved, I saw that the too much time issue is largely a cultural myth. At any rate, I could see a very clear connection between the time I spent, the money saved and the freedom I gained to choose to be at home.

This process really is about providing yourself with more life choices. You may use your increased freedom to make a different choice than I did, which is fine. Many families with two working parents, or single parents who are their family's sole source of income have used these concepts and tips to open the doors to their dreams, too.

I found myself spending a lot of my money-saver time on tasks that related to things on which we spent money for the children. I wasn't able to significantly change the house payment, but there was lots I could and did do on the child-related expenses. This book is a collection of the ideas that have worked for me. (I'd love to hear about the ideas that have worked for you. Write to me in care of *Pursestrings,* Ferguson-Carol Publishers, 36 Camino Cielo, Santa Fe, NM 87501. If your idea is used in the newsletter, you will receive a free one-year subscription or extension to your existing subscription. To receive a free sample issue of the newsletter, *Pursestrings,* send a SASE to the above address.)

At this point, four years later, I am very happy with my "job". It has translated into several hundred dollars a month that I don't need to earn and I look at every new cost-cutting idea that I incorporate into our lives as a "raise" for me. Although we are a busy household, I am free to schedule my work when it is convenient for me and arrange my days so that I am spending my life energy on the thing that is most important to me: nurturing my children. We are also reaping the rewards of living more simply - less things to maintain, less TV, less stress.

Saving money can support many family goals. You may want to find a way to take the family to Europe, put Junior in private school, save for college or just stop living on credit cards. I suggest you use this book to look at the exciting possibility that you can reduce the amount of money you are spending on your children and still have well fed, warmly and attractively dressed children, who are provided with toys and educational materials and celebrated with birthday parties and family fun times. Throughout this book, you'll find hundreds of practical suggestions that you can begin to use immediately to slow down that tremendous flow of money going out for child-related purposes. The last chapter is written for parents, especially moms, who would like to spend more time with their kids and work less.

All those little things that I learned to do to save money added up. Don't think that changing one or two things won't make a difference - they will. They will provide a foundation for the next two things, and the next two. No one does it all at once. Here are my two biggest pieces of advice: 1. Begin. 2. Persist. Soon you will begin to notice that your finances are not quite so tight. And you will notice that you don't feel so stretched by the "craziness of more", and you may even find that your life is somehow richer than it was.

Percentage of Americans who say they
have achieved the American Dream:

those earning **less than $15,000** a year - 5%
those earning **more than $50,000** a year - 6%

quoted in *All-Consuming Passion*
The New Road Map Foundation

GUIDELINES FOR THRIFTY LIVING

In this book I have included hundreds of specific tips on how to save on child-raising costs. However, I'll never be able to tell you what to do in every money spending situation, nor would you want me to. Therefore, I'm including a list of general guidelines which you can use to help when making spending decisions.

Don't be intimidated by the idea of super-savers, people making all their food from scratch, building homes from recycled materials and giving gifts made by hand in their spare time. Every one of these people had to start somewhere to get to this point - we can look to them as inspiration that it can be done. Karen Rafferty, a thrifty mom from Downey, California, commented to me, "Lots of people feel guilty that they are not more thrifty. I believe you need to start by finding out where you are and then decide what changes you can make. Once you start cutting back, it becomes easier and more ideas present themselves. It is really a process and, after a while, becomes fun."

1. Information is powerful stuff. Learn how to research answers to your questions. A world of information is available through public libraries at no cost. Ask the  librarians to help you learn the ropes. When my friend Susan was buying a new refrigerator, she found out from Consumer Reports that one brand had the lowest rate of repairs while the brand she was considering buying had the highest! For her one hour of research, she saved herself hundreds of dollars in potential repair bills.

2. It is easier to spend less than to earn more. For every $10.00 you save, that's $12.50 (pay plus tax) you don't have to earn.

3. Stop buying things that provide the least value. If your money is spent on a low-priority item, even if it is only 99¢, you will have less to give to high-priority goals. Karen Rafferty's family has a 23-year-old vacuum cleaner that they take in yearly for servicing. Their repairman told them to buy another old one if this one ever breaks because new ones aren't built to last. Karen says they buy a few, high quality things rather than many less durable ones because "we believe that the material items we purchase should be long-lasting so that we don't abuse the wonderful resources we have on this earth." Isn't it convenient that the thrifty choice is often the earth-friendly choice as well? Remember that it is the precious hours of your life that you are trading for your purchases. Make sure the things you buy are worth every penny.

4. Cut down on waste. Why pay for something and then throw it away? We are most aware of waste in the area of food, but consider all the areas where using a lesser amount might give the same result. Try using less shampoo, laundry detergent and dishwasher  detergent and see what you can get by with. Don't pay to light rooms that don't have people in them.

5. Find ways to get the same thing for less. Examples are buying used items, buying at wholesale prices with a buying co-op, tracking sale seasons and making your own. As you begin to focus on this goal, you will compile a custom list of price cutters that is unique to your life and location.

6. Use your best resources - your ingenuity and creativity. When you are contemplating a purchase, ask yourself if you already have something that would work, if you could make it yourself or if you could use a less expensive alternative. Use your imagination and find creative options.

 **7. Set up a production line.** When you make your famous $2.00 casserole, make three and freeze two. When you are sewing hair ties for your girls, sew a few more for your gift stash. Since your set-up and clean-up time is the same, you only spend a little extra time making them. The time you save can be spent on whatever you desire - cleaning your house instead of paying someone to clean it,

playing checkers with your kids or taking a long hot bath at the end of the day.

8. Propose a trade. We have friends who are massage therapists and in the last year they have traded for $6,000 worth of products and services, including dental care and piano lessons. Almost everyone has something they can trade. Be brave and ask.

9. Is it necessary? Because my kids share a room, I have the extra consideration of available space when we are making toy purchases. We've found, for instance, that buying a doll house hasn't really been necessary. The kids have little dolls and doll-house furniture which they set up in the play space in their room and then pack up again when they are done and that's been fine for them. Other choices we might make if my girls really wanted a doll house are using cardboard boxes or making a house that we could dismantle and store.

Possessions demand a lot of our time. If we decided to buy a doll house, we would have to spend the time working to pay for it and to pay for a space big enough to store it, time to shop for it, time to maintain it and the time eventually to sell or give it away. For an individual possession, this may not seem like much, but as the amount of possessions increase, so does the amount of time invested in them. Using the "Is it necessary?" question can make your life easier in many ways.

10. Identify your priorities. For one Seattle mother, the priority is being available to homeschool her youngest two children. Even though her family takes vacations infrequently and she has chosen a lifestyle that hasn't yet enabled her to buy a dishwasher, she rates her quality of life as "excellent". "No, I don't feel impoverished," she replied thoughtfully in answer to my question, "Working toward the goal is a satisfying thing in itself. Life is not a destination, it's a trip".

THE TIME IS MONEY SAVED FORMULA

When I "hired" myself to be the family money-saver, I used one tool to help me evaluate the difference my efforts were making. The information I received by using this tool was nothing short of astounding and I use it constantly now in making choices about where to put my energy.

This tool is called the "Time is Money Saved Formula". By using it, you can find out how much per hour you are "paying" yourself (read saving yourself) to cut costs. The per hour number is useful because it is a measurement of worth that we already use to value our time.

Would you pay yourself $63.54 an hour to make pizza and open soda cans at home? I would and I do every time I make pizza for my family instead of taking it home from the pizza place. To see how I came up with this astonishing number and to find out how to use the formula for yourself, look at the chart on the next page.

We all have to make choices on how to use our time. The Time is Money Saved Formula helped me decide that hanging out my laundry and saving the equivalent of 70¢ an hour was not good economics if I then didn't have time or energy left to make supper which saves me $5 - $75 an hour. Using the Time is Money Saved Formula, I saw that stopping at one more store just to buy tuna on sale was worth $20 for 15 minutes (or the equivalent of a $100 gross hourly wage) when I bought 48 cans at once - not a waste of time after all.

While it is hard to know precisely the total amount of time I spend in pursuit of thrift, I have saved us between $7,000 and $10,000 per year since I "hired" myself for this job. This year I saved about $165 a week for about eleven hours of work per week. If I include the costs of transportation, clothes, meals out and child care I would have had to pay if I went to work for these hours, and the taxes, I find that I would have had to earn $16,312 this year, or $28.50 an hour, to take home an amount equal to what I saved. (To see exactly how I worked this out, look in Resources at the end of this chapter.)

Parents with outside employment can also use this formula very successfully to see where their energy is best spent. Fewer total hours can still yield consistent savings for the family budget, but you must be selective. For instance, you may not have time to both make your own spaghetti sauce ($5.00 per hour) and your own pizza ($63.54 an hour) so clearly, making your own pizza is the best use of your limited time.

THE TIME IS MONEY SAVED FORMULA

Here's how to figure out how much you are really putting back into the family's budget by taking cost-cutting action. For this example, I am using making pizza at home vs. getting take out to show how to use the formula. It can be used with any money saving activity on which you choose to spend your time.

- Cost of two 14" cheese pizzas and four 16 ounce drinks at a well-known pizza parlor (plus tax) . . . . $ 24.95
- Cost of two 14" cheese pizzas made at home with ingredients bought on sale during my regular grocery shopping and four drinks from the grocery store (plus tax) . . $ 3.77
- Time it takes to mix, knead and roll out two pizza crusts . . . . 20 minutes
- After the crusts have risen, time it takes to grate cheese and top pizzas . . . . . . 5 minutes

Step 1: Cost of retail minus the cost of homemade equals the money saved,

$$\$24.95 - 3.77 = \$21.18$$

Step 2: 60 (minutes in an hour) divided by the minutes you spend, multiplied by the money saved equals your net "pay" per hour,

$$60 \div 25 \times \$21.18 = \$50.83$$

Step 3: Net (take home) pay multiplied by 1.25 equals the amount the average American would have to earn as gross pay to take home that much money,

$$\$50.83 \times 1.25 = \$63.54$$

$63.54 ! - I "pay" myself for 25 minutes work at this wage every time I make pizza.

Resources

• *Your Money or Your Life*, Joe Dominguez and Vicki Robin, Viking Penguin, 1992

Here's how I got the figure of $16,312 per year. This is the amount of salary I would need to earn at an outside job to contribute an equivalent amount to our household as I do by saving:

15 hours a week x $11 = $165 per week "take home"
$165 x 1.25 = $206.25 "gross pay"
$206.25 x 50 work weeks per year = $10,312.50
To this I added the costs of working:
Transportation - $25 per week = $1250 per year
Clothes - $15 per week = $750 per year
Meals out - $20 per week = $1,000 per year
Child care - $36 per week = $1800 per year
Total costs = $4,800
$4,800 x 1.25 = $6,000
$6,000 + $10,312 = $16,312

CLOTHING

    Clothing your child can be a daunting prospect. No sooner have you managed to bring together a suitable assortment of play and dress clothes and are resting on your laurels, when you begin to notice ankle and wrist bones protruding and dresses that suddenly seem a lot shorter. Take heart. Clothing is one of the most money optional things your child needs.

Clothing Babies

There is an infinite supply of baby clothes in this world. Often, just making your desire for baby clothes known is all that is necessary to open the floodgates and bring them pouring in. Babies just grow too fast for their clothes to wear out. Dress clothes, shoes for non-walkers and newborn clothes (also marked size 1 month or size 3 months) are abundantly available as hand-me-downs, thrift store or garage sale purchases. However, like the people who are giving or selling you these clothes, you are going to have only limited use for these things.

What you really want for your newborn and young infant are undershirts and T-shirts, one-piece sleepers, and sets like sweat suits or leggings and shirts. If you are using cloth diapers, you will need diapers and diaper covers. Many retail establishments will give you a "recommended" list of clothing for baby. Ignore this - it's a sales tool. Get the basics during yard sale season, wait to see what you are given and then fill in as needed. (You may be given baby items stained with formula or baby food. Try soaking these in a non-chlorine bleach before you give up on them completely. Note: For some reason, formula stains are much harder to remove than breastmilk stains. As far as I'm concerned, that's another brownie point for breastfeeding.)

> Carseats may be available for free or just a small fee through your local health or police department. For a list of programs in your area, write to:
> National Highway Traffic Safety Administration Washington, DC 20590

About Diapers

As you move toward a more frugal lifestyle, you will definitely want to consider using cloth diapers. Disposable diapers are packaged in amounts that seem to last roughly one week (more for newborns with quantitites decreasing as the child gets older). The price for a week's worth, however, stays the same. In my area, a one-week package is about $11.00, or $47.63 a month. Let's compare that with the cost of diaper service - $50.00 per month - about the same. However, the cost of washing diapers yourself is $1.60 per week, or $6.93 per month.

✦ **Diaper service.** With my older daughter, I had diaper service for two years. When I began investigating this choice, I was surprised to find that *you don't have to wash out the poop!* You put the diaper, poop and all, in a plastic bag and at the end of the week, hand it back to the diaper service. Yuck, you say? Well, how different is that from rolling up the diaper, putting it in the trash and giving it to the sanitation workers at the end of the week? Same grossness factor.

Babies who are still being exclusively breastfed do not have stinky poop. However, the consistency of breastfed or formula fed baby poop is pretty mushy (don't you love this paragraph?) until the child begins to eat solid food, hence many people's revulsion at cleaning a baby's poopy diaper.

✦ **Disposables.** As my daughter reached the age of two, I concluded, independently of her, that she would soon start using the potty. So I switched to disposable thinking the end was so near I might as well see what it was like. As you can probably guess, she didn't start using the potty until she was three years and a day old (this was the day she had proclaimed for herself). I found that using paper diapers was really no more convenient than having a diaper service and it created a lot more trash and things to lug in from the car.

✦ **Washing diapers yourself.** By the time I had my younger daughter (5 years later) I was ready to try using cloth diapers and washing them myself. At the time, we lived in a tiny apartment with no washer or dryer, while we built our house. Initially, I saved the sack of soiled diapers and handed them to the diaper service each week. I finally decided it wouldn't be much harder to take that sack with me to the laundromat each week - and it wasn't! I brought them home clean, but wet, and hung them up in the arid southwest sunshine for an extra disinfecting boost.

 This may sound like a lot of work, but it really wasn't. Once a week, I spent 10 minutes extra putting the diapers in the washer and taking them out and an extra 15 minutes hanging them out on the line. Using the Time Is Money Saved Formula (p.15), I can see that it was definitely worth my time. Each washer load cost $1.50 plus about 10¢ of laundry products ($6.93 per month). Diaper service at $50 per month minus my monthly cost of $6.93 left $43.07 that I was saving for 108 minutes of work per month. That's equivalent to earning a gross hourly salary of $29.61. My daughter didn't care what kind of diapers she wore, but she and I firmly agreed that we wanted to spend our days together. This is one of the hundreds of small ways we made that happen.

✦ **Savings.** I bought diapers and diaper covers new and it took me about nine weeks to recoup their cost. We used them for two and a half years. Since then, I have seen both diapers and diaper covers at yard and rummage sales, especially those that specialize in items for children. My local diaper service holds one of these every year - look and ask around in your area. Some diaper services sell "discards" that are slightly frayed or stained but still have a lot of wear left. For a good deal on new diapers, check out Dundee Direct. They sell new diaper "seconds" (for instance, the topstitching may be crooked) by the pound at a price that is less than half of new. (See Resources at the end of this chapter.)

The very least expensive option new is to buy a dozen diapers, diaper pins or clips and nylon (*not* plastic) pants. I used size large even on my wee babes - the elastic in legs and waist fit them for the entire time they were in diapers and they grew into the rest of it. With this few diapers, you'll have to run a load of diapers through your washer every day.

You have some options to deal with the poop: flushable, rayon diaper liners (however, they raise the cost of using cloth diapers), soaking, rinsing them in the toilet (what our moms did, bless their hearts - now there's a tool made for this that keeps your hands out of the water), or simply throwing the diaper, with anything sticking to it, in the washer and doing them all at the end of the day. The last is an option that a lot of people I know use successfully.

✦ **Eeew!** I'm including this detailed and highly entertaining instruction on dealing with poop because, as a veteran of cloth diapers I know that it is the single largest thought in people's minds when they think of cloth diapers. Please remember, if you're just now on the way to parenthood, that one of the gifts of having children is the ability to see things that used to make you squeamish and not bat an eyelash. Or, in other words, get over it.

✦ **Bleach?** Let me add a word about stain removers. Bleach is good for stains, but hard on fabric. As long as you know your diapers are clean, they are OK to use. Why spend time, energy and money on making diapers cosmetically perfect? Hot water, detergent and sunlight will kill the germs. And unless you are having a really unusual parenting experience, there won't be a large group of people offering to change the baby's diaper and therefore in a position to pass judgement on their appearance.

OK, that was the bottom line (pun intended). Now, the wardrobe for the rest of your baby's childhood.

The Used vs. New Debate

In my opinion, it's parents who have the power to determine a family's attitude towards the wearing of used clothing. If your children are objecting to this idea, take a look at how you may be presenting it to them. A shirt brought home from a yard sale, given with an apologetic, "I know it's not new, but..." is bound to meet with rejection. The same shirt, given with a flourish and a "Look what I found!" is much more likely to be accepted. If parents can communicate their belief that secondhand clothing is fine, and connect that to the family's goals, children will hop on board. My kids understand that spending less on clothes has a direct connection to more parental time at home, and they like that. Our family philosophy is that we are using our heads and our savvy to do well in the world of necessary material goods.

Our culture right now dwells on appearance to an extent that I think is neurotic. We've all had the experience of finding a person with a negative attitude unattractive, even if he or she was wearing the latest fashion. I'm sure that you, like me, know people that you want to be with no matter what they are wearing. Children have these same experiences and you can help bring this into their awareness by focusing your comments about people on their character rather than on their clothes.

That said, I'd also like to point out that it's practically impossible to go into a child's closet and tell what's bought new and what is secondhand, unless that item just came home from the store and hasn't been washed yet. Another consideration is just because it's new doesn't mean your child will like it. I sometimes take my girls to a department store so that I can get an idea of what their tastes in clothing are and while browsing, I estimate that they like about half of the clothes we see there (possibly less). Using this information, I choose secondhand clothing (or let them choose) and I would say that the positive responses I receive to the things I bring home from yard sales / thrift stores are in the 85-90% range. If your child is in the throes of desire for new clothes like his or her friends', give the kid some options, similar to your own, about what needs to be done to come up with that money. Explain to them the family's financial goals and ask

them if they are willing to do with less in another area. If your child is old enough, offer to give them the money you were going to spend anyway on the less costly choice and let him or her make up the difference in order to buy the more costly choice.

Buying Children's Clothes at Garage Sales

Garage sales, one of America's unique gifts to consumerism, are the places that you will find the best value for your dollar in children's clothing. At garage sales, you get quality, style and dirt-cheap prices. There are also many things that you will have to pass over in order to get the good stuff. Also, at a garage sale, unlike a department store, you can make an offer. Say you are looking for clothes for your son to wear

next fall. You've taken his measurements (and have them with you), have determined he'll be about a size 10 and you find a sale with a good selection of clothes in that size. Before you gather up a handful, pick up one item of clothing and ask how much it is. If your day is being blessed by the garage sale angel

and everything is 25¢, just get the items you need. I don't usually bother to bargain on 25¢ items. However, if the seller says, "Jeans are two dollars, shirts one dollar," then you might get a couple of pair of jeans and four shirts and say, "Would you take five dollars for all of this?" She will say yes or make you a counteroffer. Don't be shy about this - it is the norm rather than the exception at garage sales.

If you hit a garage sale with good clothes, but high prices, walk away. Believe me, America is still the land of abundance and the clothes are out there for 25¢, 50¢ and $1.00. My exceptions are jeans in excellent condition, shoes in excellent condition and something that is exactly the thing my child has put on her wish list.

✦ **When to get there.** The time you should try to get to garage sales is the opening time on the first day of the sale. Conversely, extremely good bargains can be had in the last two hours of a garage sale, especially on rainy or really hot days. Stock your car with a map (I use the one from last year's phone book) and a snack.

✦ **Best sales for kid stuff.** For children's clothing, the best sales are often multiple family sales, rummage sales that are fundraisers for schools and speciality garage sales for children's items, like the one run every 6 months by my local diaper service. To give you an idea of what you might find, here's my list from the four yard sales I went to one Saturday: a Hanna Andersson shirt, 25¢, a set of cotton, girls long-john style pajamas, 25¢, a pair of sandals, 50¢, a headband, 25¢, a pair of snow boots, $1.00, and a swimsuit, 25¢.

✦ **Stay in the bidding.** Try this trick that one of my garage sale customers taught me. If you see an item that you want, but can't get the price down far enough, take a piece of paper and write down a description of the item, the price you want to pay, your name and phone number. Hand it to the seller and tell him or her that $X is as high as you want to go and if the item hasn't sold by the end of their garage sale, please call you and you will come by and pick up the item and pay them. This works well for everybody - they won't sell it for less to another person and the seller has something to fall back on if it doesn't sell.

Thrift Stores

Thrift stores have approximately the same assortment of merchandise garage sales have, but they charge more for it. The advantages is that they are open regular business hours and have a constant supply. Most thrift stores also support worthy causes and you can feel good about contributing to them with your patronage. Additionally, my local thrift stores have a wider selection than is usually available at any one individual garage sale.

Most thrift stores will not bargain with you, but they do have sale days. A common sales technique of thrift stores is to have "bag day" when you can fill a bag for, say, $5.00. This can be a good deal if you can find a bag's worth of usable child-size items. Call around to see what sales policies your local thrift stores have. If they have bag sales, ask if they are on a regular day. If so, you can go in a day or two ahead and get an idea of what's available. You'll need to be one of the first there on the sale day, however.

Consignment Stores

For more expensive brands of children's clothing in excellent condition, check out consignment stores. They usually have cream-of-the-crop used merchandise at prices that are higher than thrift stores but lower than retail stores. This is a good place to sell your kids' clothes in good condition, too.

Hand-Me-Downs

Hand-me-downs are another excellent source of clothes. There are lots of people who are not interested in having a yard sale. Some people only want new clothes - be happy to let them provide you with great used clothes. So what if their new clothes look the same as ours after three washings? They're happy - we're happy.

ANNUAL COST COMPARISON *

RETAIL   ALTERNATE

	RETAIL	ALTERNATE	
3 pair jeans	$47.85	$2.00	1 hand-me-down from sister, 1 hand-me-down from friend, 1 yard sale pair
5 tops	64.00	.75	2 hand-me-downs, 3 from yard sales at 25¢ each
2 skirts	33.90	.50	1 hand-me-down, 1 yard sale
1 dress	48.00	3.50	thrift store
1 sweater	23.00	1.00	yard sale
2 hair bows	5.00	1.50	made by mom with craft store materials
1 pair pajamas	12.00	0.00	hand-me-down
8 pair panties	12.00	7.75	bought new, on sale
8 pair socks	8.00	6.50	bought new, on sale
3 pair tights	7.50	2.70	1 bought new, on sale, 2.20, 2 yard sale, 25¢ each
1 pair sneakers	31.00	1.00	yard sale
1 pair dress shoes	37.00	3.00	yard sale
1 pair snow boots	22.50	1.00	rummage sale
1 coat	49.95	3.50	thrift store
1 pair gloves	4.95	0.00	hand-me-down
1 Christmas dress	42.00	10.00	made by mom
1 summer dress	18.00	.50	yard sale
2 short sets	29.90	10.00	mom made shorts, child helped decorate matching T-shirts
1 swimsuit	14.95	.25	yard sale
TOTAL	**$511.50**	**$54.50**	

*Basic girl's wardrobe. These are actual prices seen at department stores and yard sales in 1995.

You, yourself, may be a source of great hand-me-downs for friends. I give most of my youngest child's clothes away after she outgrows them, to a mom who has provided me with many beautiful perennials and bulbs from her garden. We don't have a deal - it's just a result of stepping into the circle of sharing. Once you are done with kids' clothes, let them go! Give them away or put them in your own yard sale and help to insure there is plenty for all.

To find sources for hand-me-downs, assess the families that you know. Maybe you can make a trade with a family. For instance, you could hand down your older daughter's clothes to their slightly younger girl, and they would give you their son's hand-me-downs for your little boy. Still, sometimes all you need to do is ask, "What do you do with your children's clothes when they outgrow them?" to open a channel for hand-me-downs. In my experience, it makes people happy to know their clothes are going to someone who can use and will appreciate them.

Other Sources of Less Expensive Clothes

✦ **Family clothing exchange.** This is a variation on hand-me-downs. Several families get together, perhaps with a potluck, and bring their outgrown clothes to trade. You can do a toy exchange at the same time if you're brave.

✦ **Flea markets** are a mixed bag, but can be a good place to do the equivalent of several yard sales in one stop. It's fairly easy to identify the people who come every week. They probably will not have merchandise priced in the range you are

looking for. Stick to the folks who have obviously just brought their garage sale type items over to the flea market to sell. I have a friend who is an avid flea marketer and she has found great bargains on toys, purses, shoes, furniture and even computer software.

✦ **Retail sales** are good for things like socks and underwear. Good brands can sometimes be found at dollar-type stores, but even department stores like Sears and K-Mart have semi-annual "stock up" sales where multi-packs of socks and underwear are priced as low as any other retail outlet I have found. The boys department carries the same sweat suits as the girls (colors may vary), but usually at a lower price. Of course, wait for sales and comparison shop. My library has several books with details about seasonal sales and how to get bargains retail. I rarely choose that option myself, because it costs more, so I'm not going to cover it here.

✦ **Outlets.** The only time an outlet store is a bargain is when you compare it to buying the same item for full price in a department store. If you've decided your little one *must* have a certain brand of clothing, an outlet store is for you. I must emphasize, however, that this is the antithesis of frugal thinking. (And you will be surprised how many Osh Kosh and Polly Flinders items you see at yard sales.) However, outlets are acceptable options for teens who want specific brands (and are supplementing the purchase with their own dollars).

✦ **Sewing.** Sewing clothes can be a big money saver if you can get fabric inexpensively and use basic patterns several times. Yard sales are a good source of fabric, both by the yard and from voluminous clothing. Little girls' fancy dresses are one place where the cost of the retail item is so high that it may make economic sense to sew it yourself, even with fabric from the fabric store.

HOW ONE FAMILY MAKES IT HAPPEN

Ceu Ratliffe is a woman with a mission. She wants her family to be living proof that five people *can* live on a teacher's salary. (Her husband teaches at the local high school.) More than that, she wants her kids to know that each person is at the helm of his or her own ship. Ceu models this attitude for her children with her can-do approach to life and believes that practicing thrift has great benefits for her children. She claims, "The level of self-control necessary to be successfully thrifty creates self-reliance and self-esteem in kids."

One way this family saves money is by cutting down on little trips in the car. "At this point," Ceu says, "I have to have three good reasons to get in the car." Another way is by making sure that when they do drive, there are snacks and drinks from home available so that they don't need to buy them as they do their errands.

Like many thrifty families, Ceu's thinks that thrift is not deprivation, but a way of being smart. One of the results of putting thrift in such a positive light is that her kids actually prefer hand-me-downs to new clothes when they come from older, admired friends. This family's home is a happy home, with frequent celebrations, art and shared family projects. The kids have a few durable, store-bought toys, a few lovingly handmade toys, lots of dress-up clothes and the great outdoors. Ceu says, "The kids are doing well and our quality of life is great."

Consider Having Fewer Clothes

Sue Hodgson, who is homeschooling her seven children in St. Louis in a small house, doesn't believe in having surpluses. "My kids have seven days worth of clothes, plus one or two sets of Sunday clothes," she says, "They really don't use more than that." Whatever they don't use is given to Goodwill or to friends. Sue never buys baby clothes, or for that matter baby food, baby formula or baby furniture. She has created a network of hand-me-downs so that they rarely need to buy kids' clothes. Sue has found used children's items abundantly available. "We think of ourselves as living off the fat of the land," she adds.

Before You Shop

Before you go to even one yard sale, rummage sale or thrift store, assess your kids' clothing needs. Have you ever brought home a shirt (it was such a steal at 50% off!) and realized that your child didn't really need another shirt? Go through your children's current clothes and list anything they need now (including color and size). Next, see what they will need for next season. Write that down. Take their measurements, including the length of their foot. Manufacturers' sizes vary. Put this list in your car or purse so you will always have it with you.

✦ **Sorting and storing your acquisitions.** If you don't already have any clothes put away for next season, begin now to plan ahead. With my two  daughters, I keep two or three big plastic trash bags to handle each of their clothing stashes for future use. My older daughter receives hand-me-downs less frequently, so I buy further ahead and look harder for things for her and I have a bag for things that will fit her someday, but not this year. For each girl, I have a bag for the next season (winter or summer) which includes clothes that I think will fit them in that season. I usually try to include clothes on the large side, because for a couple of years I would find several items in the "future" bag that my child had outgrown. So now I know that my brain refuses to accept the fact that my children will actually grow that much and I compensate by putting in clothes that look too big. Finally, I have a bag into which I throw all current acquisitions, unsorted. When we get out clothes for a new season, I sort the current acquisitions into now, next season or someday piles. Then I pack up the next season and someday bags and have an empty current acquisitions bag ready to receive more clothes as we get them. With this system, I can bring home a garage sale purchase, mark it on my purse list, and stash it without much ado on my part.

✦ **How far can you take this?** As a result of buying at garage sales, thrift stores and receiving hand-me-downs, I very rarely need to buy new clothes for my girls. I usually have so many things for the younger that I give away clothes that would fit her, but that she just doesn't need. For instance, this spring we picked the best fourteen dresses and let the rest go. (She's into dresses.)

The most frequent purchases I have made new are shoes, socks and underwear. My older daughter's grandparents buy her a new down coat about every other year, which is handed down to her sibling. Our total expenditure per child is now $50-$75 per year.

What About Socks and Shoes?

Ralph Nader, the consumer advocate, has made only one major purchase of socks as an adult. He noticed, when he was in the Army, that Army socks wore like iron. Eventually, he became a civilian and needed to provide his own socks so he tracked down a source for those fabulous socks and bought several pair, all in the same color. Twenty-plus years later, in an interview, he reported that he was *still using those same socks!* He has never had to sort socks and he has never had to throw out a good sock because the mate has a hole.

Now here's a guy using his head! The interview went on to detail other frugal things Nader does and pointed out that he does this in order to do the work about which he feels passionate. OK, maybe everybody's not going to be inspired by a Ralph Nader sock story, but, really, why aren't we all doing this? If your kid spends 98% of his or her time in jeans and sneakers, buy socks in the same style and color and you'll be spending less time shopping for socks and less money as well.

✦ **Used shoes?** On to shoes. Shoes are so expensive and parents need such a never-ending supply of them that any alternative to retail is worth checking out. My kids wear mostly used shoes, but the majority have very little wear. We also receive hand-me-down shoes in various states of repair (I also wear garage sale shoes, when I can get them.) For an excellently researched response to the health concerns people voice about used shoes, order issue #55 of the *Tightwad Gazette*. For shoe repair, order #53. (See Resources.) Basically, there is nothing to indicate that wearing used shoes harms one in any way. We've certainly had no problems. As a matter of fact, my kids are wearing much higher quality footwear than they would be if I had to buy it totally new!

When you shop garage sales, rummage sales and thrift stores for shoes, take your child with you, or at least their foot measurement in inches. Shoe sizes vary widely. Give preference to shoes with least wear on the soles and with the best looking toes. Some repairs are easily accomplished with a glue gun or Shoe Goo (available at sporting goods stores). I've gotten some great deals on shoes that just needed a little touch up and were otherwise practically unworn. To replace shoelaces in children's shoes, figure the approximate size needed by counting the total number of eyelets in each shoe and multiplying by three. Also, powdered cleanser and elbow grease makes a huge difference on sneakers. Use saddle soap and polish on leather shoes.

A Few Other Things to Consider

✦   **White gets stains.** As you look at clothes, new or used, remember that dark colors are much easier to maintain and will have longer lives as good-looking hand-me-downs. We don't want our children to look always somber and dark (although teens will sometimes *choose* this look!), but an indigo T-shirt with a shining face above it is hardly dreary.

✦ **Teens.** Speaking of adolescents, teenagers and their clothes are a ticklish issue, but most kids' wardrobes are built around a core of basic shirts, T-shirts, jeans and sneakers. Take your teen garage-saling with you or provide a basic clothing allowance and let them earn the difference. Many parents are amazed at the difference that spending the dollars earned by one's own sweat makes in a person's spending habits. In addition to taking care of your own budget, you are teaching your kids about something they'll need to know when they are on their own.

✦ **T-Shirt decor.** T-shirts are really perked up with acrylic or fabric paint. This is not just for girls - cut up sponges into geometric shapes and let your children of both sexes use them to decorate a shirt or two. Acrylic paint needs a piece of cardboard behind the fabric to keep it from soaking through to the other side of the shirt. It also needs to be heat set, using a press cloth between paint and hot iron. Fabric paint does not need heat setting. Both should be allowed to dry for about 24 hours. Paint manufacturers usually recommend turning the shirt inside out to wash it. Buy three or four colors of fabric paint when it is on sale. It should last for several projects.

Great things can be done with T-shirts and applique. This is especially easy using a Wonder-Under type fusible web. Fabric stores sell this in the interfacing department and will give you instructions with it. After fusing an applique to the shirt, seal the edges with fabric paint or zig-zag around the edges.

Another quickie girl-type embellishment is ruffling the edge of sleeve or neckline. Do this by s-t-r-e-t-c-h-i-n-g the edge while you zig-zag over it. Go around two or three times until the gaps are filled in with stitching.

✦ **Remakes.** Using your own creativity, you may be able to take clothes that are too big and alter them or artfully cover up a stain that would otherwise make an item unwearable. This type of clothing is a "remake". Remakes are fun and take very little money although they do take some time.

Tee remake : Neck and cuffs ruffled and horse appliqued over stain on front of shirt .

Another fun remake is a baby romper, which can be made out of a larger size sweatshirt. Here's the idea for those of you who can do simple sewing without a pattern.

Old sweatshirts can also be recycled into over-the-head bibs.

You can often find dresses with voluminous skirts at a yard sale for 50¢, which can provide fabric for any child-size project you care to put your hand to. The sky is really the limit here and you can have fun thinking up ways to salvage unusable clothes. Crafts stores are full of ideas, but remember that your goal is to end up with a garment for less money than an equivalent one you could buy, used or new.

So don't buy $10.00 worth of craft goodies just to salvage a shirt. (I do crafts as a hobby and I constantly need to rein in my tendency to rationalize a purchase as a good deal because I'll be saving money. Be really honest with yourself, and then, if you want to buy something because it's fun and it fits in with your hobby budget, you'll have made the decision in a clear way that you can feel good about.)

You, Too, Can Do This

Again, I live in a town of 60,000 and do not have access to anything exceptional in the way of yard sales or thrift stores. You, too, will be able to find great deals when you look and use your head. I have included a lot of information here and you may be feeling a bit daunted at this point, wondering if you can do this. You *can* do this - it just takes a little consistent action towards your goal. Please remember that it took me a few years to get to the point where I only spend $50-$75 per year on each child's clothing. However, this is one area where, if you are bursting with energy and enthusiasm, or even if you aren't but you are just determined to do it, you can immediately slow your outlay of cash by getting a year's worth of clothing in one garage saling season.

Resources

• Dundee Direct. They sell diaper seconds for $3.99 per pound (8-9 diapers per pound). They have a 5 pound minimum and you must call to see if seconds are available. (800)522-3388. To compare, 5 pounds, or 40 diapers, would be about $20. New first quality diapers are about $24 a dozen.

• Mountain Air Naturals. Diapers and diaper accessories. Free catalog: 113 N. Davis, Belgrade, MT 59714, (406)388-1056, e-mail <Mtnair@aol.com>.

• The Natural Baby. Diapers and diaper accessories. Free catalog: (800)388-BABY.

• After the Stork. Low cost, basic, durable kids' clothing. (800)333-5437.

• The *Tightwad Gazette* will no longer be printed after December, 1996. Back issues should be available for $ 1 each from RR 1, Box 3570, Leeds, ME 04263.

The great thing in this world is not so much where we are, but in what direction we are moving.

Oliver Wendell Holmes

HOW ONE FAMILY MAKES IT HAPPEN

"Building a reservoir of sweet memories and certain love is the best protection for kids as they grow up and face the challenges of living in the world." So says Karen Rafferty, whose impetus for learning thrift was the birth of her son. "Once I held my son in my arms, I knew I could never leave him and return to work. At the same time, I knew that we could never afford to continue our pre-child lifestyle on a single income." Karen attained her goal of staying home by being thrifty and by doing child care in her home. Over six years, she and her husband pared their costs until they could afford to live on one income and Karen's days are now spent homeschooling her son and continuing to do all the money-saving activities that enabled her to attain her goal.

Karen believes that it is important to do what is reasonable for your family and for the time you have available. Although she persistently takes money-saving action, there are things, like making a volleyball net out of six-pack rings, that she says she probably wouldn't choose to do.

I asked her if there were any guidelines she used to help her stick to her budget. "Each family needs to decide what their governing values are," she says, "and what vision they have for their family. Once you have these, it is easier to make decisions, because you have firmly set priorities. You efforts are naturally more consistent."

TOYS

   After acquiring hundreds of little plastic toys and selling
them again at yard sales, I have formulated my strategy of toy
purchasing. Never spend more than 10 cents on such a toy,
but do buy them to provide short-term fun and little treats
throughout the year. Save your money to invest in toys and
games that will provide year after year of play value and will
survive to be handed down to your other children. An
example of this is Legos. Over the years, I have bought sale-
priced Lego sets as birthday and Christmas gifts until we now
have a sufficient supply to build a small town, if my children
so desire. This works not just with Legos, but any add-on
assortment of building toys, blocks, collections of things like

horses, cars or doll house furnishings or whatever your child loves. Here are the advantages for saving your money for this type of toy: durability, versatility, the toy just gets bigger and better, and you don't have to create a new storage space for it.

✦ **Simplify.** If you are seeking to simplify your life, consider having fewer toys. The average young girl in the U.S. owns eight Barbie dolls. The average young boy owns thirteen G.I. Joe Action figures. There is a limit to the number of toys with which children can really play. Sue Hodgson, a mother of seven, has a system to curtail toy chaos. Each child has one box and is welcome to fill that box to the top. The overflow of toys goes down in the basement. After six months, Sue goes through the toy box. Any toy that hasn't made it back upstairs to any child's box goes to the thrift store. In this way, she is able to have seven kids supplied with toys and still have a semblance of order. Some parents, me included, pack up extraneous toys and store them. When the current toy supply loses its appeal, pack those up and get out the stored toys.

I have bought dozens of jigsaw puzzles at yard sales and we've never found one with more than two pieces missing. Ask if the salesperson knows if they are all there. It's a good chance he or she was the person who put this puzzle together. Also, open the box and roughly divide the pieces into piles that are small enough to estimate in number. For instance, if it's a 500 piece puzzle, divide it into five piles and see if there's about 100 pieces in one. This will save you from buying a puzzle with a large number of pieces missing.

✦ **Yard sales.** The single best source of toys is yard sales. When you get to a yard sale, you can easily scan the offerings to see if there are any child-related items in the bunch. You might also check for art supplies and books that you'd like to add to your children's library. When you do find one of the many, many yard sales that is offering toys, look through them carefully. Check puzzles and games for missing pieces. If there's a defect, assess its repairability, and if you think you could fix it, go ahead and get it, if it's a good price. In fact, point out the defect to the salesperson. He or she might just give you a large discount. You will not believe what you find in America's yard sales. To mention a few, I have found American Girl paraphenalia, My Little Ponies, PJ Sparkles, Discovery Toys, Fisher-Price, Little Tykes, loads of board games, Tinker Toys, Lincoln Logs, several varieties of dolls, Disney stuff by the armload, Barbie stuff by the armload, china tea sets and handfuls of Legos and Duplos from the bottom of the free or 5 cent box. We have gotten toboggans, stick horses, doll house items and bed tents.

Babies need a basketful of unbreakable toys they can't swallow, yet small enough to hold. Garage sales are the place to get these at rock bottom prices. I think it's nice to have 25 or 30 of these (a few for the car, a few for the diaper bag) and in those quantities, one can easily save $50 by getting them at garage sales.

✦ **Little things.** It's important to be alert for "little things" as you buy for your children at yard sales. Little things are those small objects that parents are called on to provide several times a year. They are stocking stuffers, Easter basket items, party favors, treats on Valentine's Day, New Year's Day, even Halloween. They are the

Toys to Look for at Yard Sales:
• Toys, games and books in nice enough condition to be given as Christmas or birthday presents to your kids.
• Toys and games for less than $1.00 that are incomplete or have worn packaging, but that your kids will love anyway. One example is a Monopoly game with a frayed box that has all its pieces and is 50¢.
• Puzzles
• Little things to use for stocking stuffers, party favors, Easter baskets, etc.
• Dress-up clothes
• Baby clothes tiny enough to be used for baby dolls
• Tambourines, simple flutes or recorders
• Magnets

things you might want to tuck in your child's lunch as a special treat or leave under their pillow after a hard day. Over the year, these little things bought at full retail price add up to a chunk of money that you, clever shopper, can avoid spending. They don't need to be expensive or extreme. With two children, I tend to buy these things when I see them in multiples of two. These are things I've found at yard sales for 5-10¢: little packages of mints tied up in net with a ribbon and silk flower decoration (left over from a wedding shower), tiny pencils (doll size), doll cups and saucers from Mexico, pin cushions, little sewing kits, 3-inch yarn dolls (ten

of these in a plastic bag for a quarter), polished rock assortments, jewelry, small packs of playing cards, modeling dough molds and multitudes of miniature plastic toys.

While I've been buying for girls, there are plenty of little things that would interest boys, too. Christmas may seem a long way off when you are yard-saling in your sandals and shorts, but you will thank yourself when you need that stash of little things.

✦ **Replacement parts.** To get replacement parts for sets of toys, try calling the manufacturer. Many toy companies provide parts for free or for a minimum fee. (For a list of phone numbers, see Resources at the end of this chapter.)

✦ **Rechargeable batteries.** Do you feel like you are constantly buying batteries? Consider setting yourself up with rechargeables. Over the long run, you will save many times the initial purchase price of the rechargeable batteries and the recharger. Some rechargeable batteries don't hold a charge very long and eventually have to be replaced themselves, so I recommend that you get high quality rechargeables, available from companies like Real Goods (see Resources). Although high quality batteries are a little more expensive, Real Goods' batteries are guaranteed to last forever and will hold a charge longer, so I think it's a good value.

HOW ONE FAMILY MAKES IT HAPPEN

Susan Hubbard and her family (name changed) live on 30 acres outside a small town in New York. Her family has a big garden that provides much of their food and their country home is furnished with many antiques. Susan's husband is a medical professional and she runs a home business. Their life seems idyllic and outsiders assume they must have a large income to support themselves in such a style.

The truth, however, is that since their children were born they have lived on a reduced income and have become masters of frugality. Most of the family's clothing is bought used and their beautiful antiques are auction bargains. When their washer died, Susan put an ad in the local giveaway paper and another reader called to offer a free one if Susan would pick it up. (She did!) The kids get videos at the library instead of renting them and Susan spends her Friday and Saturday summer mornings getting first pick at yard sales.

Susan laughingly told me about a recent conversation she had with an acquaintance, who was listing her own money woes. Turning to Susan, she said, "You're so lucky that you have plenty of money." Susan agrees that the fruits of her labors are visible and that she does have a good life, but she points out that she and her husband made a lot of that happen in the time *after* they stopped having "plenty of money". For her and her family, living on less has not meant living without.

✦ **Buy a toy, skip the burger.** If your child insists that he or she must have the current fast-food toy and you are actually considering buying a child's meal to get it, ask if you can buy just the toy. Both my local Burger King and McDonald's managers have told me that toys can be sold individually (they are under $1.00), but it's up to each store to set that policy.

✦ **Toy-lending libraries.** Many communities now have toy-lending libraries. Ours is located in our local community college. It was originally set up for child-care providers, but is now open to individuals also. Each library has its own guidelines. My toy-lending library signs out up to four toys for a month at a time. The selection depends a lot on when you get there. We have always found something of interest. This is a good way to get play time with bigger or more expensive toys. I recommend that you wash them before you let your kids play with them, since many little hands have been playing with these toys.

✦ **Treats while shopping.** Do your children ask you to buy them something each time you are out with them? Realize that parents create this situation by getting little treats on every outing. I certainly created this expectation with my first child. I was shocked when I added up the amount of money leaving my purse for little things here and there, so I explained to her that we were going to have more treats at home and not get treats at stores. The first time she asked for a treat in a store, I gently reminded her that we had gum at home and she could have some when we got there. After that, I basically ignored treat requests or talked about the treats we'd have when we got home. Soon, she didn't ask anymore and my younger daughter has never learned this behavior. This does require having a treat at home, but even popsicles or muffins with sprinkles will qualify.

✦ **The cartoon factor.** Another move which will drastically cut down on requests for advertised toys (and cereal) is cutting out Saturday morning cartoons. I know, it's soooo tempting and easy to have that hour or two for sleep or privacy on Saturday morning, but you pay a price. Try an art activity instead. Or, at the very least, watch movies on the VCR. Cartoon watching will have an especially big effect in the months before Christmas, so be really vigilant then. (How many times has your child asked Santa for a $50 toy he or she saw on TV and then played with it only twice after Christmas morning?)

Advertising creates artificial desires and children are not yet sophisticated enough to recognize advertising for what it is. It's so much more satisfying for everybody if you give your children gifts they'll really enjoy. The chances of them asking for things in which they are sincerely interested are much greater if they haven't been exposed to the advertising that accompanies cartoons. Believe it or not, my children have to think pretty hard to come up with their list of Christmas wishes. To me, that demonstrates that their toy and entertainment needs are being abundantly met (without Saturday morning cartoons).

Making Toys

That said, there are so many low-cost and easy toys you can make, your child could have an abundance of toys even if you never purchased a single one. A good portion of my kid's toys are of this variety and just as dearly loved. Following are several ideas for make-at-home toys and there are lots of library books dealing with this topic. (I always love to receive ideas on low-cost homemade toys that are a big hit with kids. If you have one to share, send it in care of *Pursestrings*, Ferguson-Carol Publishers, 36 Camino Cielo, Santa Fe, NM 87501. If your idea is used in the newsletter, you will receive a free one-year subscription, or extension to your existing subscription. To receive a free sample issue of the newsletter, *Pursestrings*, send a SASE to the address above.)

✦ **Dolls.**   Dolls are important to young children's play, whether the child is a boy or a girl. They use them to be like Mom and Dad and to translate the world down into a manageable size. For a young child, this is much more easily done with a baby doll than with a Barbie doll. Children don't really need a lot of dolls, but more than one is nice so that they can create "families", and have them relate to each other.

The most basic doll is a hankerchief, with a cotton ball-stuffed head, a neck cinched with a rubber band and hands and feet made from the knotted corners of the hankerchief. (You can also cinch the waist with a rubber band, if you like.)   Is there a two or three-year-old in your house? Make one of these up and see how much time and attention is lavished on it. Give the doll its own blanket by cutting a square from another piece of fabric.

A more elaborate doll can be made from socks and fabric scraps and stuffed with more fabric scraps, yarn scraps, old pantyhose, polyester fiberfill or wool. Wool is nice because it makes the doll become slightly warm as the child holds it and it seems more babylike. Wool yarn or wool fabric scraps work fine. (If you use wool, remember when you wash the doll to use cold water and let it air dry.)

To make a doll with arms and legs, take an old tube sock and lay it out so that the body is the foot and the legs are the ribbed part. Turn your sock inside out and mark the approximate location of the legs. You can usually mark the legs so that the ribbing starts about where knee socks would be on the doll's legs. (See illustration next page.) Sew the legs seam now while the sock is inside out. Leave 1" unsewn on the inside of one leg so that you can turn and stuff the body. Carefully turn the sock body right side out. Now, using a long

pointy instrument like a chopstick, stuff the legs and the
body. Cinch the neck tightly, using thread or floss.

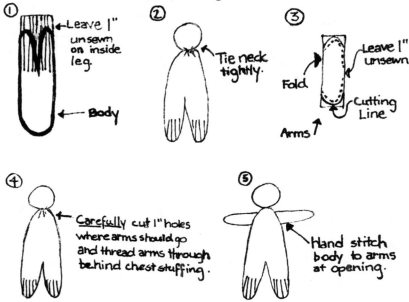

① ←Leave 1" unsewn on inside leg. ←Body

② Tie neck tightly.

③ Fold Leave 1" unsewn Cutting Line Arms↑

④ ←Carefully cut 1" holes where arms should go and thread arms through behind chest stuffing.

⑤ Hand stitch body to arms at opening.

To make the arms, use another sock or the leftovers from
your first sock, if there's enough. Estimate the length of one
arm. Double that measurement and add the width of the
dolls chest. Make a rectangle that length and approximately
3 inches wide. Fold it, wrong sides together, the long way.
Round the corners on the ends so that they will be more like
hands. Sew, wrong sides together, leaving a two inch opening
in the center of the long side. Turn right side out and stuff.

Now you have all your pieces. To insert the arms, cut
half inch holes on each side of the body at the spot where it
looks like an arm should be sticking out. Carefully thread
your stuffed arms through the holes behind the chest stuffing.
Add any more stuffing that you need in the chest area
through the arm holes. Finally, hand stitch the armhole
openings to the arms and stitch the leg opening closed. You
have a doll! This is an easy project that can be done by a
novice seamstress and all the seams can be done by hand if
you don't have a sewing machine.

To make hair or a hat, see illustrations, next page.

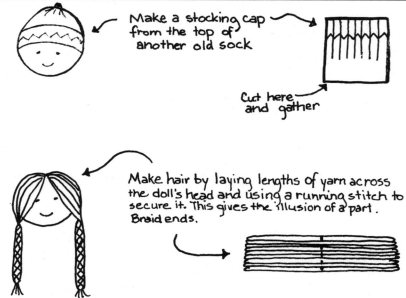

Make a stocking cap from the top of another old sock

Cut here and gather

Make hair by laying lengths of yarn across the doll's head and using a running stitch to secure it. This gives the illusion of a part. Braid ends.

I must confess, I love to make dolls. When I gave my first handmade baby doll to my toddler daughter and she loved it up, my heart just melted. There's an element in homemade toys that money just can't buy.

✦ **Doll Clothes and Accessories.** To dress baby dolls that you have made or acquired from yard sales, begin by looking through your old clothes that are ready to go to the thrift store. Use the sleeve and stretchy cuff from an old sweat shirt to make a skirt for baby (the cuff is the waistband). Hem to the right length. Use the other sleeve to make a pair of matching panties. To do this, again use the cuff as waistband and cut the sleeve fabric to panty length. Sew the front and back together in the crotch area and hem the rough edges. Instead of a skirt, if you scoot the cuff up across baby's chest and add a couple of ribbon straps, it can become a sundress. To make a cape, measure down 8" from your sweatshirt's neckline, all around, and cut. Cut a slit down the front and attach ribbon ties. (You may have to pare it down a bit to fit your doll. Size before attaching ribbon ties.) Don't limit yourself to just sweat shirts. Sometimes the cuff to an old blouse is just right to fit around the doll's waist, or

ribbon ties for shoulder straps
sweatshirt cuff
sleeve of sweatshirt
turn up hem and sew

Sock. Use stretchy fabric. Sew right sides together and turn.

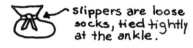
Slippers are loose socks, tied tightly at the ankle.

would fit if you moved the button just a bit. Let your child go through your give-away clothes and come up with ideas, too.

With just a smidgen more sewing, old socks can be transformed into doll tights or leggings. Turn them inside out and measure from the stretchy top down. Make leggings the length of your doll's waist-to-ankle measurement plus a half inch (for hemming). Doll socks are really just tubes of stretchy fabric with the toes sewn closed. For slippers, make them a little loose and attach a ribbon tie to the back ankle. Tie tightly on the doll's ankle. Doll size scarves are simply squares of silky fabric, hemmed. They can be used as head scarves or tied artfully about to make a summer blouse for baby. Begin to look at old clothes with a new eye for doll clothes possibilities. Of course, those of you with more advanced sewing skills may want to buy a pattern and stitch up a whole wardrobe. Any of these options is much less expensive than buying them retail.

Other sources for doll clothes are garage sales. Look here both for true doll clothes and for tiny newborn baby clothes which will fit some baby dolls.

◆ **Blocks.** Blocks are one of those toys that will be played with over and over for several years. A good set of blocks can be pricey. One way to make your own is to get 2" x 4" wood scraps and saw them into pieces 2"-4" long. Be sure to sand them very well. Another style of blocks is tree branches cut in short lengths. These work fine if the child has some planks to bridge the "stumps". This style is good for creating woodland scenes and Robin-Hood style forts. At a friend's house, I saw her son playing with cardboard boxes of all sizes that had been glued shut and painted or covered with magazine pictures. He was having a great time, building high towers and knocking them down.

Some families save all their cardboard milk cartons and let their kids use them like blocks to create structures that are child size. In catalogs that sell to child-care centers, you will see beautiful (and expensive) lightweight wooden blocks, sized 1 foot x 1 foot and 1 foot x 2 feet. They come with 1"x12" planks in lengths short enough to remain sturdy when they are bridging the distance from one block to another. If you have room to store this building toy and the skills to make it, it will light up the eyes of your child on Christmas morning and be used by him or her (and any little brothers and sisters) for years to come.

✦ **Dress-up clothes.** No matter how many other toys your child owns, he or she will enthusiastically make room for dress-up clothes. We have two big wicker baskets full and they attract every young guest we have. About nine years ago, I bought six 45" squares of cotton gauze in different colors. They are all still in use and have been used more than any other single toy that we own. They can become capes, scarves, shawls, slings, baby blankets, "traveler's" bedding, tents, turbans, 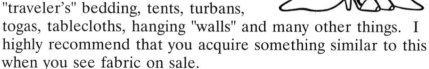 togas, tablecloths, hanging "walls" and many other things. I highly recommend that you acquire something similar to this when you see fabric on sale.

The rest of the kids' dress-up clothes are yard sale finds and adult cast-offs. There are two or three capes that were used for Halloween costumes, a felt crown I made for one year's birthday girl, a wedding veil I made in response to another birthday request, etc. Grandma gave them some old hats when she was moving. Things collect easily for dress-up with a very little amount of money. Be prepared for some wild fashion shows, menacing masked invaders and foreigners of uncertain origin to come parading through, and for this low-cost activity to entertain your children for hours.

✦ **Music makers.** This type of toy might also be called a
noise maker, depending on your perspective! Whether it
sounds like music or noise to your ears, it sounds like fun to
children. Oatmeal boxes make fine drums, toilet paper tubes
can be filled with beans or rice or gravel to make shakers,
gourds make good shakers. Use two of the scoops that come
with powdered laundry detergent to make a shaker by putting
the open sides together, throwing in a few dry beans and
taping the two together with duct tape. Bells sewn onto
elastic are great for ankles. If you can find a box that is small
enough to fit one end in the child's mouth (something like a
candy bar size, with flaps on each end - chewy candies or
gum chiclets come in these), he or she can make a great
"tooter" by just blowing air from one box end (open) to
another end (closed). Many of us did this ourselves as
children. If you didn't, I bet you can find a friend to
demonstrate.

   Supplement this collection with low-cost music makers: a
kazoo, a harmonica, a triangle. As you go to garage sales
look for tambourines, simple flutes and recorders.

✦ **Counters.** A counter is any little object that can be sorted.
Teachers call this sort of thing a math manipulative. They
can be bought in sets of several different colors and several
different animals or shapes. You can make your own with
buttons, tiles, marbles, nuts in their shell, beads, painted
popsicle sticks, painted rocks, shells, juice can lids with
various things glued to them, colored paper clips, even
crayons. Children three to six enjoy sorting. Size and color
are obvious categories, but you can vary it. The rocks, for
instance, can be big, small, various colors, polka-dotted,
striped, painted with pictures of alive and non-alive things,
smooth, rough, and measured for size categories (such as the
1"-2" category or the "it can fit in this box, but not in that
one" category). Ceu Ratliffe, mom of two kids at counter-
loving age, took all the peach pits she had left after canning
season, soaked them in bleach and dried them in the sun.
She reports that her kids use them for scooping and pouring
from one container to the next, as well as for counters.

✦ **Magnets.** Children of all ages are "drawn" to this toy. This is another item to look for at yard sales. They can be purchased in packages at the hobby store or ordered from speciality science supply stores.

✦ **Cardboard boxes.** Sometimes we forget how easy it is to provide the props kids need for play. A plain old box, big enough to climb into, can be a car, airplane, baby buggy, or horse corral.

✦ **Sponges.** I often see packages of 10 sponges on sale for $1.00. These can be cut into shapes and used for soft blocks, given to a little one for imaginary play or used by kids to wash their toys, windows, or themselves, all of which can actually be fun in itself.

✦ **Felt boards.** Take a 24" x 24" piece of cardboard and cover it with flannel. Cut out people, animals and other shapes from felt. Younger kids love these and older kids might get into the action, too. My older daughter spent an hour one day recently arranging free-form snippets of felt into a beautiful overall design.

✦ **Office kit.** Put paper clips, rubber bands, little erasers and any other little office-related item into your old film canisters. Add a rubber stamp and stamp pad, a sheet of stamps like the ones of animals that come free in some junk mail, some envelopes and a few pencils and you're in business. Office supply stores sell tiny envelopes for pennies each - a few of these are nice, too.

✦ **Stilts.** When you buy mushrooms or tomato sauce in giant cans (see the Food chapter), save the cans. Turn them upside down and have your child stand on top of them, one foot on each. Punch a hole on opposite sides of each can (near the top) with a nail. Thread lengths of sturdy string through and tie them so that they are hand height for your child. By pulling the string tight, the child can walk on the cans. This takes a little practice, so do it on grass at first.

✦ **Bowling.** Use old plastic soda bottles with a little dirt in the bottom as bowling pins. Pick a ball from the ones you own.

✦ **Sticks, rocks and mud puddles.** These are sometimes the best toys of all. Nichoe Lichen, mother of two active boys, thinks her kids are having the most fun when they dig a hole and then pour some water in it! These props form the basis for an endless variety of play. Needless to say, don't let small children be unsupervised around any pools of water.

Resources

• *Easy to Make Cloth Dolls and All the Trimmings,* Jody Davis, Williamson Publishing Co., 1990, $13.95.

• *The Doll Book*, Karin Neuschutz, Larson Publications, 1982. Soft dolls and creative free play. You may have to get this one from a Waldorf school bookstore.

• Real Goods, (800)762-7325. High-quality rechargeable batteries and other energy-savers by mail.

Replacement parts for toys:	
Playskool	800-752-9755
Fisher-Price	716-652-8402
Mattel	800-421-2887
Little Tykes	800-321-0183
Lego / Duplo	800-422-5346
Brio	800-558-6863
Milton Bradley (many games)	413-525-6411

Advertising teaches that pain can be handled by buying and consuming products. There's big money to be made in creating wants and then encouraging that these wants are needs, even rights.

Mary Pipher
Reviving Ophelia

ENTERTAINMENT AND EDUCATION

I began this section as two separate chapters, but I kept running up against items that could be entertainment or education. What kind of message do we give our children when we separate fun from learning? Instead, I have combined the two topics and included dozens of ideas for low-cost play and learning into one chapter. May these ideas provide you and your children with many happy hours!

Begin by sitting down and looking at all the areas now taking your money that are related to children's entertainment and education. I'm not talking about tuition here, I'm talking about computers, books, "learning experiences" and other things you think they need to round out their education, as well as entertainment such as Nintendo, movies, treats at the mall, etc. Be sure to include big yearly expenditures such as the Christmas Nutcracker performance, the state or county fair, the Halloween party, etc. As parents, this is where a significant percentage of our money is spent. Fortunately, it's also an area where there are many alternatives and a lot of room to use your creativity instead of your cash.

Free Entertainments

Simple, low-cost events can be just as fun as more expensive ones for kids. Here's some free entertainments to which kids under 12 respond enthusiastically:

✦ **Old photos.** Look at pictures of the kids as babies and toddlers and tell them the funny things they said.

✦ **When I was a kid ...** Tell stories from your childhood. List the things you didn't have that our kids now take for granted (VCR's, computers, touch-tone phones, pizza delivery, yogurt in every grocery store).

✦ **Abracadabra.** Do tricks of illusion (get a magic book from the library). I have yet to see this fail with kids of either sex.

✦ **String games.** Nice for quiet interludes. Look in Resources at the end of this chapter or in the library for good books on the subject.

✦ **Scoop and pour.** Sit a young child down outside with a tub of birdseed and an old laundry detergent scoop and let them scoop and pour. Your local birds will help the spills disappear within a day. Be sure to keep your tub covered or it will all disappear within a day. This also works well with untreated seed corn from the feed store or bags of dried corn from the food co-op. Kids can move this around with toy bulldozers and it can even be used inside on a hard floor because it is not so hard to clean up.

✦ **Cheer your team on.** Watch sports in person, not on TV. There are usually children's and adult's leagues whose games are open to anyone who wants to watch.

✦ **They're off!** Go to the horse races. While this may bring up images of cigar-chomping shady characters, most horse races attract a wide range of people, including many families. If you go in for only the last race or two of the day, you probably won't be charged, especially if you indicate that you are there so your little horse enthusiast can have some fun.

✦ **Move to the beat.** Turn your living room into a disco. Push back the furniture and put on some music you can't sit still to.

✦ **Ready for takeoff.** Go to the airport and watch the planes take off. This was a favorite activity for my brother and father when we were little (and it still is!).

✦ **"Exotic travel".** Go to the train station and watch the trains pull out. They probably won't let you actually get on the train without a ticket, though.

✦ **See the world.** Ride the bus around your city. While you will have to buy a ticket, it's usually quite inexpensive.

✦ **How do they do that?** Go to the fire station, the bread bakery, the bottling plant and see how things are done. Call ahead to find a time that's convenient for the business. Even adults find this interesting.

✦ **Stick weird things together.** When you get a package cushioned by cornstarch packing pellets, pass them on to your children. If they dampen the ends, the pellets will stick together and can be used to make weird and fun creations.

✦ **The blue cow flew over the purple nose.** Make your own "ad-libs". These are stories with blanks where key words should be. Without letting your child hear the story, ask him or her to supply a word. After you've filled in all the blanks, read the story aloud. It's hilarious and silly. Here's an example: Somewhere over the (noun), skies are (color). (Plural noun) fly over the (noun), why, oh, why can't I? Your child supplies the noun, color, etc. It might end up like this: Somewhere over the boot, skies are violet. Hands fly over the dog, why, oh, why can't I?

✦ **Make a time capsule.** Have every member of the family contribute one thing that illustrates life today and pack it in a watertight container, like an old coffee can. Mark "Time Capsule - 1996" on it and stash it in a safe place like your attic. To be dramatic, you can bury it, but be sure to write down its location. Make plans to dig it up in 25 years.

✦ **Have a Chinese New Year celebration.** Chinese New Year falls in January or February. Make stir-fry for dinner and have fortune cookies for dessert. Decorate with paper lanterns made from old magazine pages.

Fold page in half and make cuts 1/2" apart. Unfold and form into a circle, taping edges. Add a handle. Hang a few on a string.

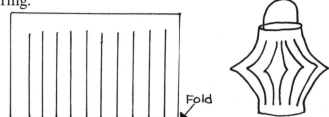

Fold

✦ **Become a hobo.** Tie your child's lunch up in a bandana on a stick and let them eat it in the backyard. For real fun, rig up a lean-to or pitch a tent. Actually, just pitching a tent in the backyard is usually enough of a novelty in itself to stimulate several hours of creative play.

✦   **Stink-a-thon!** Participate in the National Rotten Sneaker Championships. To get details on entering your extremely worn out sneakers, write: Rotten Sneaker Coodinator, Odor-Eaters Insoles, P.O. Box 328 RSM, White Plains, NY 10602. (I couldn't stop myself from imagining that some mom of an adult child got a phone call saying, "Guess what, Mom, I have a new job! I'm the National Rotten Sneaker Coordinator!)

✦ **Make a paper teepee.** Make a frame with long sticks or dowels. Cover it with newspapers or butcher paper taped together. Paint designs on it if desired.

✦ **I walked 10 miles in the snow every day.** One family has a fun tradition. When all generations are gathered around the table, Grandma will ask, "Who has a story?" Then one of the adults tells a story from his or her childhood and the children guess whether it is true or not.

Outings

There are so many interesting things in the world to see and do. Some are expensive, some we might do as an occasional treat, but many, many are very inexpensive if not downright free. I once made a list of every free event for a month in which my family might be interested. There were twenty-seven! Obviously, we didn't go to twenty-seven events, but it made my choices very clear to me. Before taking the gang out to see a movie, look around to find the lower cost alternatives, which they might enjoy just as much. Movies will always be available on video.

✦ **Listings.** To find listings of events in your area, check the free papers geared to parents. If you don't have one of those publishing in your area, look in the daily newspaper's events calendar.

✦ **Other sources.** Call the museums, bookstores, libraries and colleges to see what they have going on. They may offer to put you on their mailing list. While you are calling museums, ask if they have a free day or a reduced fee day for local residents.

✦ **PTA.** This school organization sometimes sponsors free carnivals or puppet shows.

✦ **Zoo and museum.** Yearly memberships to places such as the zoo and local museums can really cut the cost of admission if you go frequently. They sometimes have allowances for the member to bring childrens' friends, too, under the membership.

✦ **Performances for kids.** Offers are often made to public school students by community music and theater groups to attend a certain performance of a play or concert for free or at low cost. I have always asked if we, as homeschoolers, can take advantage of these offers and have never been turned down. Last year, a local orchestra group sponsored a famous violinist and gave free tickets to music students. My husband and daughter attended a concert on Friday for free and on Saturday the tickets sold for $12.

✦ **Go flying.** For a special outing, contact pilots working with the Young Eagles Program. They are offering short airplane rides free to kids 8 - 17. (See Resources at the end of this chapter for how to contact a pilot in your area.)

The Public Library

This is where I'm going to give my biggest pitch for the
public library. In my family, we read for enjoyment and so
the abundance of books at the library is wonderful; however,
libraries also sponsor story hours and movies, reading-
assistance programs, have videos and music and books on
tape to lend (and, in some place, art), often have audio-visual
equipment available, and have all the latest magazines. If
there's a book you want to read that your library doesn't
have, you can fill out a purchase request or an order for
inter-library loan (for more expensive or out-of-print books).
At my library, there's a magazine exchange area where
people leave magazines free for the taking. You can't
guarantee that a certain magazine will be there, but you'll get
to read things you've never even heard of. Children's
publications are left here, too. Not long ago, I got a whole
year's worth of National Geographic World.

    The children's librarian can be an extensive resource
person for you. He or she can direct you to books your
children might like (for instance, if you've got a Goosebumps
maniac, like I have, the librarian can show you other series in
the children's horror genre). Our children's section has a
comic book section, a books with tapes section, and a
computer loaded with games to play. It also has rocking
chairs in Papa Bear to Baby Bear size and a fireplace to
lounge around. There's even a branch library in the mall! If
my kids check out and read books from that branch, they are
eligible for free packs of stickers from the stationery store.
Please see what your local library has to offer.

    Also, there may be a few libraries besides the public
library in your town which will make lending priviledges
available to you. In my town, there are three college
libraries, the State library, the State Law library, the school
libraries, museum libraries and a library maintained by a
national parenting magazine whose office is here.

Buying Books

✦ **New books.** There are many ways to acquire low-priced books for your children's personal library. First, make sure that it's a book he or she will use more than once, or that the library doesn't have (otherwise just get it at the public library). If you buy books or magazines new (there are situations where I choose to do this), if possible buy them from a bookstore that gives 10% off on all purchases. There are several chain bookstores which offer this discount. Even in those that don't, if you are planning to buy several books at once, ask if they will give you a discount on totals over $50. One bookstore in my area has a program where children can sign up to buy books at 20% off over summer vacation. However, if I simply take the 20% card in, they will honor it, so I buy my children's Christmas books in the summer. (I like to buy them each a nice book, which is usually somewhere in the $15.00 range, so this tactic saves me $6.00 on two books.)

Don't rule out mail order books for children. Since we are homeschooling, we may buy more books than the average family. I buy many homeschool  supplies and some books by mail. Through your child's school, or local homeschooling group, you may be able to order from Scholastic, which is a sort of book club for children's books. They offer many well-known children's books at a reduced price and can have some great bargains. Also check out Dover (see Resources at the end of this chapter), which offers inexpensive reprints of classics and lots of fun volumes like paper dolls, sticker dolls, and punch-out panoramas. Some are priced as low as $1.00.

✦ **Used books.** There are several sources for used books: used book stores, Friends of the Library sales, yard sales, thrift stores and contributions from your friends and family.

Acquiring Used Books on the Cheap

Many used bookstores have a system for giving patrons credit for books they bring in, which may be used as partial (or sometimes full) payment for books they want to buy. If you have access to a store like this, here's how to get books practically for free. At every yard sale, rummage sale and thrift store where you see paperbacks selling for a dime, buy them. Also, if you get to garage sales at the end of the day, offer to buy all remaining paperbacks for a ridiculously low price (equal to a dime apiece or less). At least half the time, you'll get them. You may find a few books you want in those you buy, but that's just a bonus. You are going to trade them in at the used book store anyway, so it doesn't matter if you are not interested in these books. A word of warning: Don't buy romance novels for trade - many stores won't take them. Finally, put the word out among your family and friends that you'll take used books. Like used clothes, when you do this, there's a good chance that they will come pouring in.

So, here's an example of how it works (the percentages in your local bookstore may be different). My bookstore credits me 20% of the cover price of any book I trade in. Books for sale are marked at 40% of their cover price. I recently got a new-like edition of *The American Girl's Handy Book*, which retails for $9.95, for $4.00. But since I had taken in five books that earned me a credit of $4.00, I really only spent the 50¢ that those five books cost me at a yard sale plus the dime that my store charges on each transaction. I spent a total of 60¢ for a $9.95 book somebody had apparently looked at once. And I didn't have to make a lot of extra trips or use a lot of extra time. When I'm at a yard sale, I pick up books. They stay in a box in my garage until I take a trip to the used bookstore.

Call your child's school to see if they are getting rid of any textbooks, storybooks used in the classroom or books from the school's library. A mother from New York told me that in her state, schools put an ad in the legal section of the newspaper right before school is out. She follows the ads and has found lots of free books and even some classroom equipment that way. I have gotten some free books this way, too. It's like a treasure hunt to sift through for the good stuff.

Computers

Fortunately for those of us in quest of savings, computer enthusiasts frequently want to upgrade their computers, while their old computers are still quite adequate. We can buy them used and provide our children with some at-home computer experience. In almost every city there is one, or several, places specializing in sales of used computer equipment. When you look at new computers, ask yourself how often you are going to use all the new bells and whistles. Compare the basic features when you are making your choice. If you get the basic features you want at a good price, then you are getting a good deal.

Sometimes dealers will throw in free software when you are purchasing a computer. If the software they are offering isn't something you'll use, ask them if they will substitute another piece of software.

Right now is a great time to buy a used computer. For complete instructions on what to look for and how to stretch

your computing dollar, I recommend *Computing for Cheapskates* (see Resources).

Some sources of inexpensive software are networks or bulletin boards that allow you to download for free. Sometimes the software being offered is actually shareware. You can try it out for free for a limited period of time if you will agree to send money to the owner if you decide to keep it. Check out shareware at <www.shareware.com> on the Internet. Also look in Resources at the end of this chapter for Surplus Direct, a discount software supplier.

Many people suggest trading or buying used software. Technically, it is a copyright infringement to pass on or share software that one has purchased and used oneself, so I won't recommend it.

If your children are asking for particular software, make sure they've seen it in action before you buy it. Just as with toys, ads can make software seem different than it actually is. Computer stores will often load a game on to demonstrate if you ask. Or your child may see it at a friend's house, which is just as good. The same chain stores that give 10% off on books frequently carry software at 10% off , too.

Freebies to Write For

✦ **Free magazines.** My children really adore getting mail, especially magazines in the mail. Two free magazines (full of advertising, but with some interesting articles) are the Fox Kids Club and the Burger King Kids Club Magazines. (See Resources at the end of this chapter for addresses.) They sometimes have coupons for free french fries in them.

For almost any magazine to which you are considering subscribing, you can ask for a free sample copy. The magazine companies like to set this up as a trial subscription and you need to mail the subscription bill back with the word "Cancel" written across it if you decide not to subscribe. Getting a trial subscription is probably worth it for any magazine that you might actually subscribe to. If it's not what you want, you've only spent the stamp. It's not really ethical to ask for sample copies of magazines that you are sure you won't subscribe to.

HOW ONE FAMILY MAKES IT HAPPEN

Sue Hodgson of St. Louis, Missouri, is an at-home mom with seven children. Her family is active in their church - they tithe and are saving to send the boys on mission when they are old enough. They have two cars, both paid for, and are working toward paying their home mortgage off early. Many of us might wonder if the only way to do all this is to be wealthy! But Sue's is a middle-income family, like many in the U.S. So how do they do it?

They've done it by making certain choices about where to spend their money. Sue and her husband chose to buy a small house and to put a limit on each child's total amount of possessions. All the children have plenty of clothes and toys, but no one in this family accumulates a towering pile of possessions, so they don't need extra storage space. Surpluses (toys and clothes not being used) are given away or sold. Sue notes wryly that her kids often forgo their store-bought toys anyway to play with things like boxes and sticks and they have a plentiful supply of those.

Instead of spending money, Sue uses resources she already has to provide the things they need. For instance, when the fabric on her couch was wearing thin, she pieced together old blue jean fabric for an attractive, durable slipcover. She doesn't think of herself as a superwoman, but she is diligent in doing the things that support her priorities. Her reward for that diligence is visible in her home every day.

✦ **Freebies from government offices.**

• Consumer Information Catalog. Get the catalog by writing to P.O. Box 100, Pueblo, CO 81002 or request by e-mail at <cic.info@pueblo.gsa.gov> with the words "Send Info". There are many low-cost and some free pamphlets listed in it, such as "Helping Your Child Learn Geography" (50¢) and "Stars In Your Eyes: A Guide to the Northern Skies" ($1.50).

• U.S. Geology Service. To get their list of free publications write to USGS Book and Report Sales, Box 25425, Denver, CO 80225. (For example, they have booklets on tree rings, volcanos, map reading and rock collecting.)

• The Forest Service. They have Smokey Bear books, stickers and Junior Ranger kits. Write to Smokey Bear Headquarters, USFS, 1621 Kent St., Room 1001 RPE, Rosslyn, VA 22209.
    If you have a Forest Service office in your area, go see what else they have available. Some offices have other free stuff like pencils, and we got some great posters on different kinds of trees and wildlife, including one on tracks. Woodsy Owl materials (patches, stickers, detective and coloring sheets) are available from USDA Forest Service, P.O. Box 96090, Washington, DC 20090.

• The Environmental Protection Agency has coloring and puzzle books about recycling and pollution. Write: Public Information Center, EPA, 401 M Street SW, PM-211-B, Washington, DC 20460.

• The State Department. They publish reports on almost 200 countries. Access them by modem at (202)647-9225 or by fax at (202)647-3000.

• The Federal Reserve. They'll send your kids an entire catalog of free publications, including a pamphlet on how to spot counterfeit money (the whole topic of counterfeiting money is fascinating to most kids) and another called "Fundamental Facts About U.S. Money" telling how money is made, what all the symbols mean and how much is in circulation. Write to the Public Affairs Department, Federal Reserve Bank of Atlanta, 104 Marietta St. NW, Atlanta, GA 30303.

• The Post Office. Next time you are in the post office ask for the free coloring books they have available for children.

• DOE Conservation and Renewable Energy Line. Call to request a kids' packet. (800)523-2929.

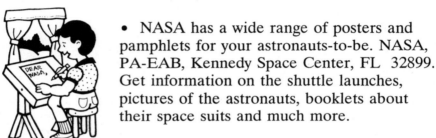

• NASA has a wide range of posters and pamphlets for your astronauts-to-be. NASA, PA-EAB, Kennedy Space Center, FL 32899. Get information on the shuttle launches, pictures of the astronauts, booklets about their space suits and much more.

• USDA County Extension Agents. Most counties in the U.S. have an extension agent. Many of those offices are quite extensive resources of free advice about gardening, canning, and homemaking. They have hundreds of free pamphlets, many on issues regarding children. To find your extension agent, look in the phone book under Federal Government, U.S. Department of Agriculture.

✦ **Others Worth Knowing About**

• Sports fans can get free packages that usually include a decal, pictures of the team and the current schedule of games. For baseball, hockey and basketball, you must write to the individual team office. For football, write to NFL Fan Mail, Box 25, Trenton, NJ 08650. Ask for the fan mail package for one team only.
• Coca-Cola stickers in several foreign languages are available from: Consumer Information Center, The Coca-Cola Co., P.O. Drawer, 1734, Atlanta, GA 30301.

✦ **Books of freebies.** It is possible to buy, or borrow from the library, books that have lists of freebie offers. Sort through these offers for the truly free ones - some charge more postage and handling than the product is worth. Look in Resources at the end of this chapter for titles of these books.

Kids' Arts and Crafts

Providing children with quality art supplies can make a big dent in a parent's pocketbook. Here are ways to give your budding artists the materials they need without spending quite so much money.

✦ **Paper.** In a home where children are encouraged to create, paper is essential. For several years now, I have had an abundant supply of free paper, given to me by a local printer. Even small printers are going to have ends of packages they can't use up and trim pieces from their odd-size jobs. Call or go by, explain what you want (the stuff they are going to throw away), and be sure to say you want it for your children. We have gotten 11"x17" sheets perfect for drawing or painting and 8½"x11" sheets of all colors and textures (including a stack of ivory linen weave paper that I use for stationery). We've also been given sheets of adhesive-backed shiny paper, card stock, trim ends in many colors and weights and tiny glossy cards, folded in half, perfect for place cards or doll-size Valentines. Check this source first!

Before I discovered printers, I found two other sources for low-cost paper. One is butcher paper by the roll, available from restaurant and kitchen supply stores. One roll will probably last you forever. It's great for tempera paint and watercolor, since it is treated to make it water resistant on one side (use the other side to paint on). It is also handy when you want to do a poster, mural or banner-size project, for a disposable table covering and to create your own wrapping paper. The cost of butcher paper is about $45 for a 1000-foot roll, 30 inches wide.

My other source of paper is the newspaper. When those giant rolls of newsprint get down to a size too small to support another print run, the newspaper replaces them with new rolls. My local paper sells the rolls for 25¢-50¢ according to the amount of paper on the roll. Newsprint is great for crayons, colored pencil or collage, but is too porous for paint and markers.

 ✦ **Crayons, markers, watercolor and tempera paint.** The best season to buy new crayons, markers and paints is the back-to-school sale season. This group of art materials are fairly inexpensive new (and on sale). Brushes are a more pricey item and worth looking for at yard sales, since brushes in several sizes and shapes can add to the fun and quality of a young artist's work. I buy new sets of crayons and watercolors for each child every few years and then pick up extras at yard sales so that we can have an abundant supply should we have a group of kids at our house coloring or painting.

✦ **Colored pencils.** There is a definite difference in the quality of colored pencils along the price scale. This is not to say that you need to buy the most expensive pencils; however, take the time to lay down some color with pencils that you're considering so that you can see if it covers well. Why spend any money at all on pencils that are going to leave the user feeling dissatisfied? Go to an art materials store that supplies professional artists (non-professionals do go in there all the time) and look at the pencils. One good brand is Berol. Most sell pencils individually, so if your child really wants a gold or silver pencil, you can buy it alone, rather than buying the bigger set of pencils just to get gold and silver.

✦ **Acrylics and oil pastel crayons.** These are appropriate for the older child. You will probably want acrylics rather than oil paints since they can be washed up with water. Buy acrylic paint in tubes at the hobby or art store (watch for the sales). Acrylic paint also comes in bottles, but it's thinner than you will need for canvases. Use the bottled paint for painting fabric, wooden decor or ceramics. Don't rule out paints and a canvas for your child - children often do incredible work when given artist level materials. It makes a nice birthday or Christmas present. Fortunately, paints are often available used because people buy them, intending to take up painting, and then only use them a few times. I have a friend who bought a box full of slightly used acrylic paints and an oak easel for $27.00. I know that everyone is not going to want to set his or her child up to paint canvases. However, I want you to know that if you decide to do it, there is a way to make it happen by using your ingenuity instead of your money.

Oil pastel crayons, known by the brand name Cray-Pas, sell for about $4.00 for a set of 12. They are not as messy as paint and children love their intense, vibrant colors.

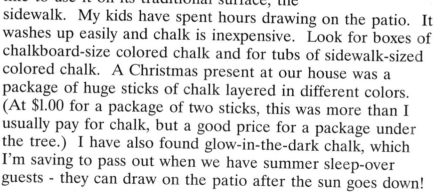

✦ **Chalk.** Chalk can be applied to paper (and set with ordinary hair spray), but we like to use it on its traditional surface, the sidewalk. My kids have spent hours drawing on the patio. It washes up easily and chalk is inexpensive. Look for boxes of chalkboard-size colored chalk and for tubs of sidewalk-sized colored chalk. A Christmas present at our house was a package of huge sticks of chalk layered in different colors. (At $1.00 for a package of two sticks, this was more than I usually pay for chalk, but a good price for a package under the tree.) I have also found glow-in-the-dark chalk, which I'm saving to pass out when we have summer sleep-over guests - they can draw on the patio after the sun goes down!

✦ **Clay and modeling dough.** Need a little time out? Give your kids a hunk of clay and some sculpting tools (a toothpick, a garlic press, a rolling pin) and let them get at it. Be sure to buy plasticene, which won't dry out. Also, cheap clay sticks to the kids hands, tools and the table so much that it is more trouble than it's worth. However, for a truly low cost alternative, make your own modeling dough:

    2 cups white flour
    1 cup salt
    4 tsp. cream of tartar
    2 Tbsp. oil
    2 cups water with food coloring or one package
      Kool-Aid added for color

Mix all ingredients together in a pan. Cook over medium heat until the dough pulls away from the side of the pan and forms a ball. Knead when warm. You can also add glitter at this stage if you want.

Begin to look at yard sales for things your kids can use to make designs in the dough. Many kitchen utensils (like melon ballers and ravioli crimpers) are fun and plentiful in the used marketplace.

✦ **Glue, glue sticks, scissors.** Get a year's worth of glue at the back-to-school sales. Give your child scissors that are sharp enough to cut well. Don't waste any money on scissors that don't cut. There are many brands of safety scissors that do cut paper just fine. One good brand is Fiskars.

✦ **Buttons, sequins, film canisters, juice lids, toilet paper rolls, broken costume jewelry, old magazines, lace and ribbon snippets.** These sorts of things will be available to you at free or practically free prices when you look and ask around. Don't go overboard and fill your garage with this stuff. Find a cardboard box and limit your collection to what will fit inside. Then, when you need a quiet hour or two, bring out your box and some paper, glue and scissors for the children.

✦ **Glue gun.** Add a low-temperature glue gun to your art supply stash. Frequently on sale at the hobby store for under $10.00, this tool can be used for repairs around the house as well as art projects. With their lower melting temperatures, they can be safely used by kids 8 and up.

A safety note: for young children, only buy art products with a CP or AP symbol on the label, which tells you that it is nontoxic. Teach kids not to put art tools or materials in their mouths and don't eat food in the art areas.

✦ **Make your own art materials.** With a few other useful recipes, you can have a choice of art materials made from items in your kitchen cupboards.

✂ **Salt dough.** Mix 2 cups of flour (not self-rising) and 1 cup of salt. Form into a ball by adding a little water at a time (up to 1 cup). If you want colored dough, add food coloring to the water. Knead for 7-10 minutes. Sculpt free-hand or use cookie cutters. If you want to hang it, make a hole with a straw. Moisten pieces with water that you want to stick together. This dough may be air-dried for 48 hours or baked at 325 degrees. Allow 30 minutes of baking time for each quarter inch of dough thickness, or until it is golden brown. If you wish, you can paint and varnish your piece when it is cool. For more nifty things to do with salt, write Morton Salt (see Resources at the end of this chapter).

✂ **Goopy gunk.** Kids absolutely love this stuff. Put a few drops of liquid food coloring or a small dab of paste food coloring into ½ cup Elmer's glue (not school glue!). Add ⅓ cup plus 1 Tbsp. Sta-Flo Liquid Starch to the glue and mix. Pour off the remaining liquid. This recipe is a bit temperamental depending on the local climate, but what you will probably get is a Silly Putty-like substance that will stretch great distances without breaking. My kids like to dangle it off our second floor loft until it stretches to the first floor. To be safe, keep it off of furniture, walls and hair. This recipe is not perfect since over time, ours always gets too sticky to play with and we have to make another batch, but it provides so much fun that I thought I'd include it anyway.

✂ **Edible modeling dough.** Mix equal parts of peanut butter, honey and instant or non-instant milk powder. This is sort of an art activity and snack rolled into one.

Rubber Stamps

Rubber stamp enthusiasts come in all ages. It is an easy way for kids to decorate their papers and cards and do free-form art. You can even get permanent ink to use to stamp on fabric. The retail price of rubber stamps is from $2.50 to $12.00 each. However, as a smart shopper, you can make a collection of stamps that you acquire for much less by buying on sale (especially after the holidays), buying pre-assembled assortments of stamps (look in Resources for the Farm Country General Store), and buying unmounted stamps and mounting them yourself.

Unmounted stamps are available from mail-order stamp companies. My favorite is Yes! Pigs Can Fly (see Resources at the end of this chapter). They offer unmounted stamps for half price. Their best deal is a grab bag of stamps where you state a preference for type of design. For instance, I stated a preference for planets, stars and angels. I got 23 stamps and rubber cushion for a total of $17.00, which is an average of  74¢ each. One was their "Deco Egyptian" stamp, shown at right. My husband, Jim, cut some wood blocks from wood scraps and glued the stamp, cushion and block together with rubber cement.

Stamp inks come in permanent or water soluable. Inks marked "child safe" are non-toxic and usually water soluable. If your child is old enough to use permanent ink, you can cut the cost of stamp pads by buying re-inking ink at the office supply store. A bottle that is big enough for multiple re-inkings is about $1.79 and comes in black, blue, red and green. For really sumptous results, use a professional ink like Color Box.

Music

There is so much wonderful children's music being made right now that you may have a hard time deciding which to get. Check out the Music for Little People catalog. (See Resources.) Also, see what your library has. Give the children's librarian a copy of your favorite music catalog and make a specific request for one or two tapes. Don't forget the option of loaning out your recordings and borrowing your friends'. With judicious buying and borrowing, you can provide your children with a rich variety of music.

Your kids can easily make rhythm instruments. Acquire tambourines and plastic flutes at yard sales. When your little one is ready for band type instruments, call around. Many music stores run programs where people donate their old instruments 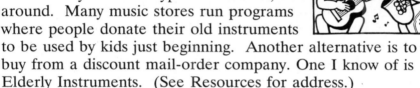 to be used by kids just beginning. Another alternative is to buy from a discount mail-order company. One I know of is Elderly Instruments. (See Resources for address.)

Games

Games are the bread and butter of children's entertainment. When we think of kids at play, we often think of them playing games. Here are some basics to get you started and don't forget board games for an evening's fun with older kids.

✦ **Bean bag toss.** Use old jeans, cut into 4"x7" rectangles. Stitch them up, wrong sides together, leaving a 2" opening in one side for turning and stuffing. Stuff with beans, lentils or rice. Hand stitch closed. You can decorate these with fabric paint or leave them plain.

Bean bags can be tossed toward baskets, boxes with holes cut in them, taped marks on the floor or just tossed back and forth like balls.

✦ **Air ball.** This is like basketball, only played with a pretend ball. Really, it's amazingly fun and can be played in the house. You can also play air baseball, tennis or football (you'll have to decide if you allow tackling in the house). It's a great way to practice moves. As a child, I got enough confidence to join in the big jump-roping games at school by practicing air jump rope at home.

✦ **Store.** Save up your old egg cartons, cracker boxes and so forth until you have a full bag. Give this to your child along with another egg carton stocked with coins. I, personally, can't see much advantage to using play money. A bag of play coins often cost more than their equivalent in the real thing and is not so easily turned back into cash. Be the banker and give out, say, $2.00 in coins on the understanding that $2.00 will be returned to you at the end of the game. Children who like to play store are of the age that is just learning about money and may need help counting to make sure it is all returned. A few empty grocery sacks and a marketing basket are helpful accessories.

A variation is playing jewelry store. For this, one gathers up old costume jewelry (which can be stored and displayed in egg cartons) and business commences.

✦ **Guess the smell, guess the shape.** When my oldest daughter was four, her favorite activity when I cooked was to go through the spice cabinet, looking at and smelling each herb and spice. If I was feeling adventurous, I would let her put together an exotically seasoned oil and vinegar dressing. We expanded this into the game where a person is blind-folded and asked to identify different scents. There are so many around your house - perfume, vinegar, oranges, pine needles, dirty socks (well, maybe not), vanilla. Of course, never sniff anything like paint or thinner - those products that have fume warnings on their labels.

When your nose gives out, play guess the shape. Gather objects into a large bag, blindfold the player and ask him or her to feel each object and guess what it is. It is not as easy as it seems.

Things to Look for at Yard Sales:

- Books for a dime or less, to trade in at the used bookstore.
- Books to add directly into your child's library.
- Crayons and watercolors if you want to own multiple sets.
- Old kitchen utensils to sculpt clay and modeling dough.
- Plastic recorders, flutes, tambourines and other rhythm instruments.

Resources

- *Free Family Fun,* Cynthia MacGregor, Berkley Books, 1994, $4.50.

- *Playing Together: 101 Terrific Games and Activities that Children 3-9 Can Do Together,* Wendy Smolen, Simon and Schuster, 1995, $10.00.

- *365 Outdoor Activities You Can Do With Your Child,* Steve and Ruth Bennett, Bob Adams, 1993, $6.95.

- *101 Great Ways to Keep Your Child Entertained While You Get Something Else Done,* Danelle Hickman and Valerie Teurlay, St. Martin's Press, 1992, $8.95.

• *String Figures and How to Make Them*, Caroline Furness Jayne, Dover, 1962, $5.95.

• *Blackstone's Tricks Anyone Can Do*, Harry Blackstone, Citadel Press, 1983, $7.95.

• *Bill Severn's Best Magic: 50 Top Tricks to Entertain and Amaze Your Friends on All Occasions*, Bill Severn, Stackpole Books, 1990, $12.95.

• Young Eagles Program. Free 20 minute airplane rides for kids 8-17 to encourage an interest in aviation. Contact the EAA Aviation Foundation, P.O. Box 2683, Oshkosh, WI 54903. (414) 426-4831. You'll be sent a list of participating pilots in your area.

• *Free Stuff for Kids*, Meadowbrook, Revised yearly, $5.00.

• *Burger King Kids Club* magazine. For kids eight years and older. P.O. Box 1067, Hiram, GA 30141. Free.

• *Fox Kids Club* magazine. P.O. Box 900, Beverly Hills, CA 90213 or <http://www.foxkids.com>. Free.

• Dover Publications, 31 E. 2nd Street, Mineola, NY 11501. An astounding assortment of low-cost books, stickers and paper villages to assemble. Write for a children's catalog.

• *Computing for Cheapskates*, Bob Nadler, Ziff-Davis Press, 1994, $12.95.

• Surplus Direct, 489 North 8th St., Hood River, OR 97031. (800)753-7877. Mail-order discount software.

• Yes! Pigs Can Fly. Box 1613, Jackson, WY 83001. Rubber stamps by mail. Unmounted stamps available. Catalogs are $3, which is refunded with orders over $10.

• Farm Country General Store. Rt. 1, Box 63, Metamora, IL 61548. (800)551-FARM. Mail order stamp sets for $5 - $10, and lots of other interesting offerings for homeschoolers.

• Morton Salt. 110 N. Wacker Drive, Chicago, IL 60606. Write for their nifty salt dough recipes.

• Kids Art. P.O. Box 274, Mt. Shasta, CA 96067. (916) 926-5076. Art materials and books for kids and groups.

• Music for Little People. Tapes, CD's and basic instruments for kids. (800)727-2233.

• Elderly Instruments, P.O. Box 14249, Lansing, MI 48901. (517) 372-7890   They carry mostly stringed instruments, both used and discounted new. For a current list of instruments available, call them or look at their home page on the Internet <http:\\www.elderly.com>.

I was rich in sunny hours and summer days, and I spent them lavishly.

Henry David Thoreau
Walden

HOW ONE FAMILY MAKES IT HAPPEN

Celeste and Kenny Epstein visit the used toy store every Christmas when shopping for their three children. They both work at Apple Computer and for years they spent everything they made. When they had some financial setbacks, they were forced to re-evaluate their spending patterns and began to discover spots like the used toy store. Since being prompted to cut their spending, they have been able to bring their finances into balance. "This experience was actually very freeing," says Celeste.

The Epsteins continue to use their frugal skills. Before they make a purchase, they research all options, using the yellow pages, classified ads and e-mail. Celeste sews curtains and Halloween costumes. Kenny looked at the expensive wooden swingset at the store and then went home and built one for $100. When they need furniture they shop at Goodwill where they recently found a couch and two chairs for $80!

Celeste's next goal is a garden expansion. She recently got the nurseryman to knock off $1.00 on each blueberry bush she bought and to let her have several flats of pansies from his "trash" pile. She has several more money-saving projects planned.

Even though their financial choices have changed drastically, Celeste and Kenny think their life is just getting better and better.

BIRTHDAY PARTIES

   Creating special celebrations and memories for my children are one of the things I like best about raising them. Birthdays parties are a great time to bring a little magic into their lives. Sure, you can hire storytellers, clowns or magicians for big bucks, but with only a little of your own creative energy, you can provide birthday entertainment with every bit as much sparkle, and with minimal cash. (And even have fun.) We have a total budget of $60 for gifts and party at our house.

There are some basic elements to birthday parties: cake and ice cream (and sometimes a meal is provided), the opening of presents, and activities / entertainment. Additionally, you'll need supplies (plates, cups, art supplies, props), decorations, treat bag / favors and party hats (optional, but enjoyed by 3 to 6 year olds). A theme may be chosen that reflects the child's interest, such as pirates, horses, or ballerinas. This is not necessary, but does provide a jumping-off point for ideas for games and decor

Again, the key is to think and plan ahead. Let's look at each party element.

Food

Food is an essential element. I usually try to serve cake and ice cream at mid-point in a two hour party. This leaves a little anticipation time, but not a roomful of hungry children. Just in case you don't know this, hungry children are NOT FUN. Cake mix is often on sale. If you can't be sure ahead of time what kind of cake your child will choose, get two kinds and chocolate icing while it is on sale (the odds are really good they'll pick chocolate icing). The extra cake will

get used in a pinch sometime. Cake mix on sale is only a little more expensive than scratch cake, however, the least expensive option is made-from-scratch for both cake and icing. Look in a basic cookbook, such as *The Betty Crocker Cookbook* for reliable recipes. Let me make a note here that my family eats mostly natural and organic foods. But I will say, with apologies to the sisterhood of whole food moms, healthy cake just does not sell well at birthday parties.

One New Yorker I spoke with, a frugal mother of two, used a bowl as a cake form for her daughter's birthday cake. A Barbie doll was inserted into the middle of the baked cake and the cake was frosted to resemble a full skirt. Her daughter loved this cake!

Birthday candles and candle holders can be re-used on future cakes - don't throw them out. It is much less expensive to get sprinkles from an ice cream or frozen yogurt store than to buy them at the grocery store. My local frozen yogurt store sells two small scoops for 50 cents, which is about equivalent in volume to the $2.00 bottle at the grocery store. Little figurines are sold in the cake decorating section of hobby stores. Alternately, you can do as I did for a 5-year-old's birthday, and sit her down with her basket of "little things" to look for a suitable frosting-immersible toy for the top. She quite happily "bathed" her purple dinosaur and arranged him on the cake. If your older child lobbies for a professionally decorated cake, explain to him or her that you have a total budget for birthdays and more money for cakes means less money for gifts. If your child understands this and still opts for the fancy cake, OK! Let them order it within the dollar limits you set.

Don't schedule a party at meal time, unless it's part of the theme. For instance, a tea party theme might include grapes and finger sandwiches, and slumber parties are hardly complete without pizza. Otherwise, opt out of meal preparation - it's less cash and less stress.

Opening of Presents

This is a no-cost activity with intrinsic entertainment value. Count on it for 15-30 minutes you can use to set up the next activity.

Activities / Entertainment

OK, here's where you use your head instead of your pocketbook. Some ideas follow to get you started. Look for more books of ideas at the library and also in back issues of *Family Fun* magazine. (See Resources at the end of the chapter.) Needless to say, use what you have and improvise. If the party plan will require many purchases, change plans.

✦ **Treasure / scavenger hunt.** Cut out map-size pieces of paper bags, burn their edges and draw a map with a permanent ink felt tip marker. (Gauge the difficulty level to the children's age.) Then wipe them with salad oil to give them a suitably decrepit look. One map per party is actually sufficient. Gather the children round and give each one a title, such as "Keeper of the Map," "Navigator," or "Distributor of Treasure". Have the children follow the map to the treasure (for treasure ideas see party favors). This could be supplemented with bandanas tied on pirate-fashion and eye patches. If you have a boat available that the children could sit in, even better.

✦ **Gold hunt.** A variation on the treasure hunt. Use pennies, peanuts (in the shell) or gold-painted rocks and hide them in a sandbox or around the yard. Provide treasure bags for their loot. Here's how to make a treasure bag with felt (if you use another fabric, be sure to finish the edges, which isn't necessary with felt).

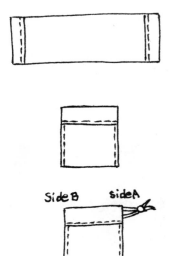

Cut one strip of felt 8"x4". Fold 1" down on each 4" end and sew in place, leaving a 1/2" channel to thread the ties through.

Fold it in half with sewn edges facing out. Sew side seams 1/4" from edge. Start seam *below* the folded over top piece.

Take two 18" pieces of ribbon or cord. Thread one piece through the top beginning on Side A and back through the top on the other side. Tie ends on Side A.

Now thread the other through the same way beginning on Side B. When you pull on the tied ends, the top should gather closed.

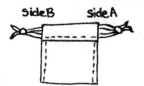

♦ **Painting with water.** This is a good outdoor activity for young children just arriving at a party. It gives them something to do while you wait for the last guest to appear. Buy a package of inexpensive foam or bristle paint brushes. Set out plastic containers of water and watch them cover everything in sight.

♦ **Mural making.** This can be an indoor or outdoor activity. Hang up a large sheet of paper or an old sheet and pass out crayons. This makes a nice memento for the birthday child, too. If you use a sheet, it can be used as the birthday tablecloth.

♦ **Water balloons.** For hot weather birthdays, exploding water balloons can be the highlight of the party. You need to buy balloons made especially as water balloons - my local party store sells 100 for $4.00. Fill them up and store them in a big tub or plastic swimming pool and cover them with a sheet so guests won't be tempted to sample a few too soon. When you are ready, let guests toss them to each other from ever-widening distances. Pretty soon, they won't be able to catch the balloon without it popping and drenching the catcher with water.

♦ **Make a village.** Go to your local appliance store and get (for free) three or four refrigerator boxes. Before party time, set them up and, using a utility knife, cut doors and windows. Two can even be taped together and a passageway cut connecting them. Provide crayons and markers with which the kids can decorate the "houses". Decorating and playing in a box village can provide hours (literally) of fun, even after the party's over.

✦ **Parade.** Get out all your noise and music makers and let the birthday child lead a parade. This can be expanded to include an activity to make shakers out of toilet paper holders filled with rice, beans or lentils, and decorated on the outside. We went to a party where the first activity was painting (with acrylic paint) banners made out of pieces of old sheet. They were left to dry during the party and then stapled to pieces of dowel. The last activity was a parade complete with banner waving and kazoo playing, and the kids got to take their banner and kazoo home. At another party during harvest season, the kids made masks and paraded around holding corn stalks. Consider, also, the time-honored "anything with wheels" event where the kids bring their bikes, skates and skateboards and decorate them, followed by a rolling parade.

✦ **Go to a ball game.** Many cities support farm teams for the big leagues. These games are usually under-attended and the management offers all kinds of deals from free entrance to give-aways to get fans to come to the games. Taking your party guests to a game can be fairly inexpensive depending on the deal being offered when you go. Of course, take your own drinks, snacks and cake.

✦ **Barbie clothes.** When I was about 10, my mom bought a length of pre-printed Barbie clothes at the fabric store and at my party we cut and sewed by hand. I haven't seen those in a while, but today's parents could create something similar by using a simple pattern (look in your library for books with patterns). Use your fabric scraps or buy a couple of 25¢ garage sale items with plentiful fabric and cut them up. Sew or hot glue sequins, trim and fasteners. With a little elastic, the guests could make matching hair ties for their dolls, or themselves.

✦ **Capture the flag.** This is a great party activity when you have a substantial number of guests coming. Parents can play, too. Divide your group up into teams and give each team their own armband color (strips of cloth tied on each person's arm). Look in a library book for suggested rules for this game. Try to find a spot that has sufficient hiding places. One round of Capture the Flag can take over an hour, so this might be the only activity your party needs.

✦ **Face painting.** This activity is a perennial favorite. We use solid shortening mixed with paste or liquid food coloring for paints. These will leave faint colors on the skin, but then so will most face paints from the store. With all face paints, try to keep paints away from neckbands and collars.

✦ **Puppet show.** Hang a curtain across the doorway and give your guests fancy tickets for the show. Paper bags full of popcorn add pizazz. The puppeteer, of course, will have to be prepared with a good story beforehand, but the puppets themselves can range widely. Use the ones you have and supplement those with sock  puppets or even paper plates on a stick. Success depends on the presentation, not the puppets. Most kids will sit still for a 15-20 minute story.

✦ **Sprinkler.** While this may seem mundane, I have yet to see it flop on a hot day. Have the guests wear their swimsuits. You can show up with your homemade juice popsicles or frozen watermelon pieces right before the end of the party. This is a ready-made situation for painting a watercolor mural (on a sheet of paper hung out of sprinkler range). Paint and get wet, paint and get wet.

✦ **Blowing bubbles.** Another simple activity that children love. Use it while you're waiting for all your guests to arrive. Here's the bubble recipe I use, passed down to me by a babysitter: 1 Tablespoon glycerin, 2 Tablespoons Joy brand dishwashing soap, 1 cup water. Glycerin, however, has gotten fairly expensive. Try substituting 2 Tablespoons of Karo syrup for the glycerin. Whichever you choose, it's a good idea to compare the cost of supplies to the cost of getting little bottles of bubbles when they are on sale four for $1.00. If you want some bubble wands, you'll probably have to acquire a few of these bottles of bubbles anyway.

✦ **Solving a mystery.** This is an activity around which you can build a theme party. It's basically a twist on the scavenger hunt idea. Start ahead planning this - it requires a little thought power.

Alyssa Reid
Detective Agency

Here's what we did. Add your own creative genius. While the kids were decorating their paper treat bags ("detective kits"), and making their "detective badges" (they decorated circles of card, we glued on pin backs), I took all the presents and hid them on top of the washer in the utility closet. Next, I gathered the guests all together and explained that they were responsible, as a team, for solving any mysteries that came up during the party. I had another mother as an accomplice, who "discovered" the presents were missing and that a clue had been left behind. She wondered out loud about this until the kids finally caught on. Then they grabbed the clue and were off.

Clues were messages written in rhyme. This is fun - you won't be submitting these poems for publication. My husband, Jim, wrote the word REFRIGERATOR on a large piece of paper and wired it to a tree branch some distance from the house. Then we set a pair of binoculars on the window sill. Here's the clue: "Use your eyes and you will see/ A message out upon a tree." I think it's really more fun for the guests if they have to do some thinking to get the answer. One clue was written in code, another in invisible ink. (Invisible ink is milk used on white paper. The paper is held above a candle flame and the message appears. Close supervision here is a *must*.) One message needed to be read with a magnifying glass. The final clue led to the presents and was followed by the opening of the presents.

Decor for this party included large dolls and stuffed animals wearing false noses, mustaches and glasses. The invitation, designed on our computer and adorned with clip art (available at most public libraries) was made to look like a business card for a detective agency with my daughter's name as the agent. The other side was a "Detective Wanted" ad, with details of the party time and place and a space for the guest's address. We copied these, postcard size, onto card stock at the copy store. At this writing, postcards are 10 cents per invitation less expensive to send. Go for postcards, if possible, or hand deliver invitations to friends you see frequently.

✦ **Dress-up.** To make playing dress-up special enough for a party, there must be at least one fancy-type hat for each child. These are often available at yard sales and thrift stores, so stock up ahead of time. Lay out or hang all clothes and accessories so that they are easy to see. Follow with a tea party. Adding tea cups and a teapot to the cake and ice cream should be sufficient.

✦ **Grooming.** This is definitely a gender-typed activity. Parents and willing adult friends style hair, give manicures and supervise jewelry or hair-bow making. This activity can be very successfully combined with Dress-up.

Art Activities

Art activities are a natural at birthday parties. I have seen simple and even complicated art projects completed successfully. Art is a good first activity and usually provides a finished product for the child to take home.

✦ **Origami.** A favorite activity of those nine and up, origami, or paperfolding, can be used as the first party activity or saved for later. Any lightweight paper will do and libraries always have a book or two with basic instructions.

Boxes and animals are popular with kids and, of course, the guests can take them home.

✦ **Decorating T-shirts.** Have each guest bring a blank T-shirt. You provide **one or two types** of the following adornment. (Put a piece of cardboard between the front and back of shirt.)

   1. Acrylic paints and brushes or sponges (guests could cut their own shapes). Acrylic paint needs to be set with a hot iron after drying. Use a press cloth between paint and iron. The paint needs to dry for 24 hours before ironing, so you might provide written instructions on heat setting for each guest to take home to his or her parents.

   2. Plastic jewels, sequins, trim and fabric glue to keep it all affixed in the washer

   3. Fabric paints, fabric crayons, or fabric markers. (Paint needs to dry 24 hours.)

   4. Fabric applique adherred to the shirt with Wonder-Under brand heat-sensitive interfacing (instructions come with it) and the edges sealed with fabric paint.

   Any of the above projects can be done in under an hour. If the child is under seven, he or she will need a lot of adult help, but it's still possible to do it. Children really love doing this activity. The types of supplies you need for shirt decorating are often on sale at the hobby store and a little goes a long way. The only thing this isn't true for is plastic jewels - buy two or three different kinds and then give each guest EXACTLY the same amount in EXACTLY the same colors.

✦ **Puppet making.** Do you have a supply of socks without mates? Use felt scraps, glue, buttons and yarn to let the kids transform them into puppets. A couple of months before the party, get a box into which you can throw anything you think might adorn a puppet - pill bottle caps, interesting packaging, shredded tissue paper, leftover Christmas tinsel, etc. Be around with your low-temperature glue gun to help attach the decorations. If you hang a curtain across a door, you'll even have a few spontaneous puppet shows.

✦ **Pipe cleaner people.** My children attended a party where this idea was used. After the little pipe cleaner people were made, the kids were led on a woods walk where they collected rocks, sticks and leaves. Then they were escorted to a "village" where individual "yards" had been outlined with stones and supplied with little lumber scraps to be used for building a house for the pipe cleaner person. The leaves, etc., that had been collected by each child provided extra building materials. The little houses were built and played with during the party, then left for the birthday child to play with in the following week. Each guest took a pipe cleaner person home with him or her. ("That was SO fun!" my children said, when reminded of this party. Cash - no, ingenuity - yes.)

To make one pipe cleaner person, you will need one wooden bead (about 1" diameter, with a hole completely through it) and one 12" pipe cleaner. Cut the pipe cleaner in three 4" pieces. Take two pieces and thread them through the bead together. Let them emerge about 1/2" on the other side of the bead and then give them a twist, separating and flattening the very ends against the bead. Bend the remaining pipe cleaner piece in the middle and twist it around the figure right under the head to form arms.

Make pipe cleaner people before the party and have buttons, pill bottle caps, acorn caps, felt and fabric scraps, pieces of old silk flowers, etc., with which to dress them. The guests will also need markers for drawing the faces. Permanent is best - it won't run when it gets wet, but monitor permanent marker use carefully. Have an adult or older child standing by with a glue gun to make sure everything is firmly attached.

✦ **Yarn dolls.** Even older children like making these. In fact, it's a little too complicated for kids under age six. For each doll, you'll need one wooden bead (approximately 1/2" diameter), a toothpick, 4 little rubber bands, 48" of yarn, fabric scraps and a piece of cardboard 2"x4".

Break the toothpick in half and glue the end of one half to the inside of the bead, so that it looks like a head with a skinny little toothpick neck. Wind the yarn completely around the 2" width of cardboard about eight times. Slip yarn off the end of the cardboard, keeping loops intact, and secure each end of the looped yarn with a rubber band. These are the doll's arms.

Now wind another piece of yarn around the 4" length of cardboard about eight times. Like above, slip it off the end of the cardboard and secure each end of the yarn with a rubber band. This is the body and legs.

Position the arms in the center of the body/leg piece and perpendicular to it. Fold body over arms and tie a piece of yarn to make a waist. Cover toothpick "neck" with glue and push it down into doll abdomen. Draw face on bead.

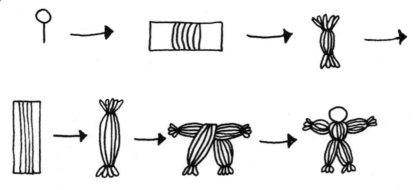

✦ **Wands.** Every wand begins with some kind of stick. This can be pre-cut pieces of dowel, old chop-sticks, or even cardboard fax paper rolls (ask an office worker to save these

for you). Cut stars and circles (about 5-6" in diameter) out
of card stock, cardboard or felt. Have the guests glue on
buttons, sequins, or old piece of jewelry and decorate with
markers.

For a very sturdy wand, make a
star or circle sandwich with two pieces
of felt or cardboard and liberally glue
the stick between the two pieces of
the sandwich. Then sew or glue the
edges of the star or circle together,
gluing it to the stick around the spot
where the stick emerges from the
sandwich. For a lavish effect, add streamers or ribbon.

Food-Related Activities

Especially for older kids, buffet style food assembly can be a
great activity. Pizza is a natural for this type of activity.
Double or triple your usual dough recipe and roll out 6" size
circles. Have the sauce and toppings available and let them
go at it.

Another tried-and-true food assemblage is the ice cream
sundae. When we did this, I was surprised to find that those
expensive syrups were neither expensive nor hard to make at
home. A little bottle of cherries also goes a long way. Use
ice cream store sprinkles (see cake decor) and whip your own
cream for topping. You get a feeling of extravagance and
indulgence, as well as an activity for your guests, for only a
few more dollars than ice cream alone. In fact, sundaes are
more than enough without cake - we had sundaes at the
weekend party and the cake on the child's actual birthday.

Field Trips

Field trips are another category of birthday party activity that
can provide your entire entertainment for the party. For a
low-cost outing, stay away from places that charge a fee.

There are many alternatives and you can adjourn to a nearby park afterward for cake and ice cream.

In addition to my suggestions, there will be places unique to your city. Look around as you do errands and flip through the yellow pages for ideas. Small manufacturers are very good tour locations. Have you ever seen Mr. Rogers find out how peanut butter, roller skates or saxophones are made? It's fascinating to children (and to adults like me). In my town, we have a candy maker, pasta makers, bakeries and an art foundry. As my children get older we may take a group to the nearby big city where there are lithographers, a famous guitar maker, a computer manufacturer, etc.

Other varieties of field trips include public service facilities (like fire or police stations), newspaper offices, wildlife and garden centers, facilities at a community college (mine has a planetarium), or public swimming pools. Even spots like car showrooms or a safe construction site can be thrilling to small car and machine fans. Check your local museums to see if they have kid activity rooms. Many are adding that feature and you can often picnic on the grounds.

Party Games

This favorite birthday activity, the party game, is basically a no-cost and fun way to entertain, especially for younger children. Go to the library (yes, again), where you will find volumes on children's games. Look it up by topic as they won't all be in the birthday party section.

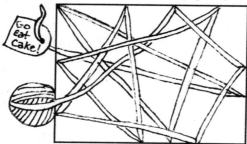

I think the kind of game, like Pin the Tail on the Donkey, where kids stand in a line to play and there's only one winner, are the least fun. Our personal favorites are two: rolling an M & M, marble or egg across the floor with one's nose (blowing a balloon with a straw is a variation on this) and the Spider Web game. To play the Spider Web game, designate one room , with no breakable items in it, to be covered by the spider's web. Take a ball of yarn and tie a small treat or a coupon for birthday cake to the end. Hide the end under a cushion or between a couple of books. Then wind the yarn around the entire room, going through slats on chairs and under tables. After you've created a good path for the child to follow, take your yarn to the door of the room and snip the end. One child will take that end of yarn and follow it to the other end.

Repeat this procedure until you have enough ends of yarn for each child to have one. As you wrap each length of yarn around the room, interweave it with the others. By the time you do it six or eight times, your room will look like it's covered by a giant spider web. (Kids' eyes get big when they see it.) To play, give each guest the end of a string and have them find the ends - all at once! It's hilarious to watch them figuring out how to unweave the web around each other's strings.

Another fun game, that older children like too, is drawing by holding a felt-tip pen with your toes. Have a go at it - it's impossible to stop giggling.

Party Favors

If you go to your party store and buy an assortment of party favors, you can easily end up spending several dollars per guest. Here's a list of favors to make or buy inexpensively:

- Tiny bottles filled with beads or glitter
- Plastic combs (can be decorated with painted flowers or glue-on sparkles)
- Little candles
- Bookmarks
- Big chalk
- Pencils/pens

- Doll-house size wooden objects (I got a package of eight wooden bowls for 58 cents on sale at the hobby store and painted a tiny flower in the bottom of each.)
- Little spiral notebooks
- Stickers
- Tiny baskets of "treasures" (polished stones, shells, etc.)
- Spiral or color change straws
- Erasers
- Fans
- Little bouncy balls
- Bracelets (beads on elastic thread - a snap to make)
- Foam airplanes (cut from foam meat packages)
- Seedlings
- Paper umbrellas (sold to put in drinks, clip the pointed end)
- Little cars (get them when they're on sale for 19 cents)
- Pictures of the guests that you have taken throughout the year
- Eye patches, pirate style (fashioned from stiff black fabric,like interfacing, and black elastic cord)

- Little plastic animals
- Gross (read wonderful) things from the bargain bin after Halloween, like green fingernail polish, fake bleeding fingers, etc.
- Cute things from the bargain bin after Easter (like packages of jelly beans, which you can take out of the Easter wrapper and repackage in plastic wrap tied with a ribbon)
- Bottles of bubbles
- Things you get as freebies, like pens, pads of paper, etc. We were at the title company closing on our house one year just before our birthday party season. They had a bowl full of pens, given to their clients after they had used them to sign the closing papers. I asked if

we could have six more to use at a birthday party and they readily agreed. After all, six more households are seeing that company's name on a regular basis when they use that pen.

- A length of good string (which you can dye an eye-catching color by soaking it in water with a few drops of food coloring in it) and photocopied instructions for a few string figures
- Little books from the thrift store or yard sales collected throughout the year
- Barettes or ponytail holders (buy one economy size package)
- Barbie kitchen items (again, buy the package and divide them among the treat bags)
- Hazelnut folk. To make this little trinket, sand the bottom of the hazelnut, if necessary, so it will stand by itself. Glue a wooden bead to the top (this makes the head). Using a 1" x 2" piece of felt, wrap it around the head like a scarf or shawl and anchor it with a dot of glue. Around the neck tie a piece of embroidery thread, or really, any kind of thread, even dental floss. She's done! Faces are optional.
- Origami cranes, suspended by a thread from a straw or thin dowel. Stand one up in each glass on the party table.
- Here's a great idea for favor bags, shared with me by another thrifty mom. She finds a drawing that illustrates the theme of the party. Then she takes the drawing and paper lunch bags to the copy store. They photocopy the drawing onto the front of the lunch bags. Guests can color the bags to please themselves.

Again, use your imagination. When you see a bag of eight or more items, all alike, at a garage sale, ask yourself if they have party favor potential. When packs of lollipops are the week's special, get one and stash it in your party box. By the time your party rolls around, you may have enough goodies to amply fill a bag without having to shop at all.

HOW ONE FAMILY MAKES IT HAPPEN

Nichoe Lichen believes that simplicity is a virtue. Nichoe, a single mom of two boys 7 and 12, also has two adult daughters. "I was raised to value simplicity," she says, "and my father always told me to put more back into the world than I take out. To me that means that if I use all my resources to consume, I won't have anything left to give."

Through her church, Nichoe's kids are able to make friends with kids whose parents have the same values. At birthday parties among this circle of friends, the guests are often asked to just wrap up something they have at home that they are no longer using, or to bring a picture they've drawn or a letter they've written. Nichoe gives a high priority to having a peer group that values simplicity and thinks of her own group as a big resource for her family. She adds, "It's great because we're all very open to passing down clothes and toys."

Nichoe is also careful to give her kids opportunities to experience the kind of play they don't see on TV. Her boys spend hours constructing things out of scrounged lumber and digging holes which they fill with water for their homemade boats. She remembers having time as a child to daydream and be in nature, so she curtails extracurricular activities like sports to one activity for each of her children. "My goal," she says, "is to have time to be humans being, instead of humans doing."

These are the favors we will have for our upcoming Cinderella's Ball party: one lollipop with a chewy center (bought three months ago when they were 29¢ for a package of seven), tiny recycled pill containers filled with "fairy dust" (glitter I got for a total of 50¢ at an after Christmas sale) and decorated with a little iridescent tinsel glued to the lid, one little pink notebook (stashed away when they were on sale for 9¢), one purple ink pen (also 9¢) and one stick of sidewalk chalk bought in a big bucket on sale. It was 10¢. They will be in fancy paisley bags that I got at the garage sale of a boutique owner whose boutique had gone out of business. They were 5¢. Total for favor bag with five favors: 44¢ per guest. They'll also be taking home with them a Cinderella "dress" - an old pillowcase given neck and arm holes and decorated with jewels, etc. (as a party activity). I collected these all year as I came across ones that were being thrown out or as I replaced mine with nicer ones, so they were all free. I bought plenty of jewels so that they can each have an identical assortment of 10 (yes, on sale). The jewels cost about 50¢ per guest.

Bags can be plain brown lunch bags, decorated by your guests or by your children before the party. White bags can often be had for a few cents apiece, or sometimes just for the asking, at bakeries. Favors can also be given in boxes that you've decorated or even baskets if you inherit several that you're willing to part with. Remember, presentation is 75% of any successful party element.

Decorations

The purpose of decorations is to impart a feeling of festivity, and to lift your party location out of its everydayness into something special. Party decor can be practically free if you put your head to it. Streamers, or their equivalent, can be made of scrap paper cut into a pattern (fringed or paper doll fashion) or cut according to the illustration. Paper can be taped end to end to give you long, room size pieces. Colorful paper like flyers or even the Sunday papers look good.

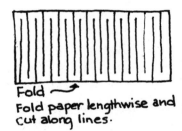

Fold ➔
Fold paper lengthwise and
cut along lines.

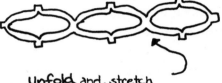

Unfold and stretch

   Also, using scrap paper, your children can make linked paper chains in any length you like. These, which you've probably seen or made before, consist of a 1" x 6" piece of paper taped or glued end to end so that it makes a circle. The next piece of paper is threaded through the first before it's taped so that it makes a continuous line of links.

   I have also managed to find crepe paper at yard sales and we have a couple of elaborate Mexican tissue paper garlands that we have used again and again for over ten years. There are many avenues to acquire or make this type of decor. As you invent new ones, please write and tell me about it!

   Balloons are an essential party element and immediately inspire a party feeling. Although my children love helium balloons, I no longer buy them for parties. For one thing, they're expensive. For another, acquiring them is time consuming and risky. Sometimes they don't all make it through the car trip or pop unexpectedly in the house, so you need to get several more than you'll need to give one to each guest as they leave. Instead, we buy large bags of balloons when they are on sale at the party store, blow them up ourselves and tie them up liberally all around the party area. We can have about 50 of these balloons for the price of two helium balloons. My children still manage to get several helium balloons a year, at store openings and other retail celebrations, for free.

   Signs such as "Happy Birthday to Ivy!", if they are big and colorful, are very pleasing to children. Many people have banner making software on their computers and would probably make a sign for you if you asked, but I still prefer the butcher paper and tempera paint variety.

Table decor is important to children and they'll probably ask to arrange the table themselves. I've found that it's not essential to have Power Ranger

plates, Power Ranger napkins *and* Power Ranger cups. Plates by themselves, along with coordinating (this could be white) napkins, give a special look that is sufficient. We have enough plastic cups with lids for a party of kids. (I've been thankful for those lids often). You can use the cups you have or your regular on-sale solid color paper cups. I have seen packages of paper plates with children's party designs on them at yard sales. If you're uncertain about whether your children will like them, buy them if they're a good price. If your children don't like them, you can always resell them for the same price at your yard sale. You can add special, but thrifty, touches by tying up a few jelly beans in plastic wrap and placing it beside each plate or one popcorn ball or any little treat that you spend pennies on.

Centerpieces need to stay low, so little eyes can see over them. Potted plants with miniature figures hidden in them provide some amused contemplation while children are waiting for the cake to be cut. Rough and ready train sets can be set up in the center of the tabletop, too, as can scenes of animals or little dolls. Please don't put anything out that it's not OK for your guests to touch. We often just skip the centerpiece - the real table action is cake and ice cream anyway.

Resources

Here are some places to look for more great low-cost
birthday party ideas:

- *Family Fun* magazine, P.O. Box 10475, Des Moines, IA
50347, (800)289-4849, $12.95/year.

- *The Pennywhistle Birthday Party Book*, Meredith Brokaw
and Anne Gilban, Simon and Schuster, 1992, $14.00.

- *Happy Birthday Parties*, Penny Warner, St. Martin's Press,
1985, $9.95.

- *Birthday Fun*, Judith Hoffman Corwin, Messner, 1986,
$5.95.

- *Origami for the Enthusiast*, John Montroll, Dover, $5.95.

Whether you think you
can
or think you can't,
you're right.

Henry Ford

FOOD

Food, glorious food! I can never hear that refrain without seeing, in my mind's eye, the little street urchins in *Oliver* spooning up their gruel. You can bet they weren't picky eaters. Today, we have such a variety of foods available to us and yet our kids sometimes do become picky eaters. Ironic, isn't it?

Well, picky eaters or not, we do need to feed our families. Food is a large percentage of every family's spending and it is another area where you can take action that will reduce the amount of money you need to spend. Following are some basic guidelines for producing low-cost, yummy meals for your family. Begin slowly, take one step at a time, and sooner than you would have believed possible, you will see your food budget decrease.

✦ **Eat together when possible.** Sitting down to eat with the family changes the quality of your eating experience and costs nothing. After long days at her job with Apple Computer, Celeste Epstein says, "We were so overwhelmed that we got in the habit of throwing food at the kids and leaving them in front of the TV." Now they set the table, light a 30¢ candle by each person's place and say a prayer. It has made a huge difference. "It really wasn't that hard," she says wonderingly.

✦ **Keep up with food expenditures.** Make it a habit to keep a list of *all* food expenditures. You must do this if you want to be able to track the decrease in your spending. This includes all stops at the convenience store, fries for the kids and so on. I include dining out in my food total, since meals out reduce the number of meals at home and vice versa. If possible, keep your receipts, too, so that you can get a picture of those items on which you are spending heavily. It makes sense to do this so that you can focus your money-saving efforts first in the areas where it will do the most good.

✦ **Keep up with prices.** Amy Dacyczyn, of *Tightwad Gazette* fame, has come up with a simple, but effective system to do just this. (For a detailed description, read her book - see Resources at the end of this 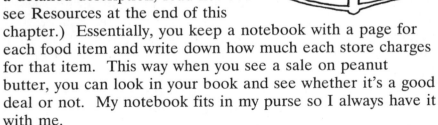 chapter.) Essentially, you keep a notebook with a page for each food item and write down how much each store charges for that item. This way when you see a sale on peanut butter, you can look in your book and see whether it's a good deal or not. My notebook fits in my purse so I always have it with me.

✦ **Bakery thrift stores.** Can you fit two weeks worth of bread (or more) in your freezer? If so, keep up with how much you spend for bread in two weeks and then go to the bakery thrift store and price an equivalent amount. Weigh your savings against the time spent making an extra stop. I buy organic bread made by a local bakery. Even fresh bread is less expensive directly from the bakery, but I make most of my bread purchases from the day-old shelves that they, like most bakeries, have.

✦ **Buy in bulk.** There are a few ways to do this so that it saves you money. One is buying from the bulk bins at your local supermarket or natural foods grocery. Most of the time (always check, though), buying here is less expensive than buying the same food sitting in a package on the shelf.

Another way to buy in bulk is to buy a lot of any product you use often that is on sale. Tuna goes on sale for 50¢ a can at least four times a year. Why pay 79¢ when you could probably find room for a case of 48 cans under your bed? Even if you have to begin small by buying two cans of sale-priced tuna instead of one, you will gradually free more and more money for bulk buying, which will free more money, etc. If I find a great sale, I sometimes buy a year's supply. We may even have enough hot chocolate mix for two years because I got it when it was a nickel a pack. Another mom I know buys cases of ready-made pizza crust at the restaurant supply store.

Do you pass by those huge cans of food, even when they are a good deal, because you think you could never use it up before it went bad? Try this: when you open the giant can, divide it up into regular size portions and freeze it. I do this with tomato sauce and mushrooms because it drastically cuts the cost per serving. This tactic, and all bulk buying yields another benefit - you really cut down on trips to the store because you have run out of something. To me, that's true convenience.

Warehouse stores can also have bargain prices. Sharing cases with friends is one way to cut on your grocery bill. Be sure to compare prices. I buy dishwasher detergent at my warehouse store because it is always cheaper, even when I compare it to sale prices, but tuna on sale is much less expensive at my supermarket.

If you have a natural foods grocery, you will probably be able to order items in case lots for a price reduction of about 10%, while supermarkets don't usually offer this option.

However, most of my personal bulk buying is done through my food buying club. Food buying clubs are groups of people who have banded together so that they can order enough food at once to qualify for wholesale prices. Jim and I have chosen to feed our family mostly natural and organic foods, so we belong to a natural foods co-op that orders from a big co-op warehouse. Although not all items are sold by the case, most of them are. Through this source, we often get organic foods for the same price that I might pay for their non-organic counterparts in the supermarket. Vitamins are also significantly less expensive from this source. (Buying organic food is more expensive overall, but I want to make the point that if you have made this a priority - and natural food sales are going up 23% a year, so there's a chance you are at least thinking about it - you can still live on less money. Reducing your food budget is possible no matter what your personal food choices are.)

Many people are not aware of the co-op option, so here is a list of warehouses across the country. If you call one in your area, they will hook you up with a local club.

Ozark Cooperative Warehouse
Fayetteville, Arkansas
(501) 521-2667
Serves Alabama, Arkansas, Georgia, Louisiana, Texas, Oklahoma, Mississippi, Tennessee, Florida, Missouri and Kansas

Hudson Valley Federation of Co-ops
Poughkeepsie, New York
(914) 473-5400
Serves most of New York, northern New Jersey, northeastern Pennsylvania, and western Connecticut

Northeast Cooperatives
Brattleboro, Vermont
(802) 257-5856
Serves New England, eastern New York, New York City

Mountain People's Warehouse
Auburn, California
(916) 889-9531
This is NOT a co-op, but local food buying clubs can order from them.

Federation of Ohio River Co-ops
Columbus, Ohio
(614) 861-2446
Ohio, Virginia, West Virginia, eastern Kentucky, Tennesee, Maryland, Washington, D.C., western Pennsylvania, southeastern Indiana, northern North Carolina

North Farm Cooperative
Madison, Wisconsin
(608) 241-2667
Wisconsin, Illinois, Michigan, Indiana, northwestern Ohio, St. Louis

Blooming Prairie Warehouse
Iowa City, Iowa
(800) 323-2131
Nebraska, Missouri, Wisconsin, parts of Kansas and South Dakota, Illinois, Indiana, Iowa, Michigan

Blooming Prairie Natural Foods
Minneapolis, Minnesota
(800) 322-8324 in Minnesota
(800) 328-8241 outside Minnesota
Western Wisconsin, Minnesota, parts of North and South Dakota, northern Iowa, and the upper peninsula of Michigan

Tucson Cooperative Warehouse
Tucson, Arizona
(800) 350-2667 outside of Arizona
(520) 884-9951
Serves Arizona, New Mexico, Utah, Colorado, Southern California, west Texas and parts of Nevada

In larger communities, co-ops are sometimes run as stores, where anyone can shop. If you join, you get a percentage off. To find out if there are any of these stores in your area, or to get information about starting your own food buying club, send a SASE to Kris Olsen, Co-op Directory Services, 919 21st Avenue S., Minneapolis, MN 55404.

It may be possible to be your own one-member club. My warehouse, the Tucson Cooperative Warehouse, requires a minimum order of $250 plus a 2.25% capitalization fee. At the $250 level, you have to pay $15 shipping, but at the $500 and above level no shipping is charged. You can order monthly or once every two or three months, and the truck will deliver your food directly to your door. The advantage to belonging to a club with more members is that you may be able to split cases with another member. My club has 40 members so I can often buy just one or two items at the case price (for instance, when six people are splitting a case of 12).

✦ **Cut down on waste.** A study of America's garbage revealed that Americans, on average, throw away 15% of the food they buy. How much does this translate to in dollars? Well, if you follow a "low-cost plan" for your grocery shopping, the USDA estimates you will spend about $106 per week on food for a family of four. Most of us are throwing away *$16 or more* worth of food each week! That's at least $832 per year. Sure, it takes some energy to keep up with what is in the refrigerator and minimize waste, but let's look at the total amount of our energy that goes into wasted food: We have to earn $1040 per year to bring home $832, we have to go to the store and buy this food, and we have to clean its slimy, moldy remains out of the refrigerator.

My friend Karen freezes all her leftovers and thaws them out for a smorgasboard dinner one night a week. Others make a list of what is currently in the refrigerator and stick it to the front. I think a weekly meal plan helps curtail waste, too. Use whatever works for you, but do it.

✦ **Garden.** If you are one of the thousands of Americans who love gardening, you can use your hobby to reduce your food bill. Be careful - spending $1,000 on gardening supplies to raise $500 worth of food is not good economics. I want to emphasize that it is not necessary to have a garden to  reduce your total food expenditure, but if you can do it, your produce costs will plummet and you'll have nutrient rich veggies to feed the kids. There's something about picking it out of the garden that makes it taste better to even vegetable-resistant children. Look in Resources at the end of this chapter for some good books to get you started.

Also consider making some of your landscaping "edible". Sue Hodgson, a thrifty mom from St. Louis, Missouri, put strawberries out in front of her house because they are such a pretty plant. Once established, landscaping plants such as fruit and nut trees and berry bushes provide essentially free food every year.

✦ **Make food from scratch.** If you are now living a time-deficient and sleep-deprived life, you may think this is impossible. Actually, it is quite possible, if you start small and cook smart.

Eating out almost always costs more than eating in and eating convenience foods almost always costs more than cooking from scratch. You might begin by just ordering water with your dinners out instead of a drink and coming home for dessert. Eventually you can, if you want to, get to the point where almost all of your food is made at home from scratch, and you will reap the financial and nutritional benefits.

Progress Report?

Joan Dye Gussow, a professor of nutrition at Columbia Teacher's College, has gathered statistics that indicate that the modern family indeed does have a decrease in food preparation time. However, we have an equal increase in the time spent food shopping, so our overall time expenditure is the same.

When we were building our house, I would pack up the kids and do the chores that come with housebuilding: visit the tile store (again!), take the bid sheet by to the roofers, pick up more paint chips, etc. By lunch time I was ready for a break and the baby was soon to be napping in her car seat. Sometimes I would stop at a fast-food restaurant for take-out because we were all tired and hungry. However, after doing this a few times, I realized that I was spending at least 15 minutes sitting in line before I even got to the window. When I timed the whole thing and realized we spent 20 to 30 minutes on "fast-food", I decided I wasn't doing myself that big of a favor. I wonder, for those of us who have children, if eating out is really a time and energy saver.

I highly recommend that you make a menu plan for the week. Every minute that you spend planning will save two (or more) later on. It will also enable you to avoid that 5:30 p.m. "I'm hungry and tired so let's eat out" decision. Eventually, you will be able to make more spur-of-the-moment dinners from your pantry and freezer, but to begin you should have a plan. That way, your dinner ingredients are on hand, and all your tired brain has to do is look at the menu. When you are planning, include one dish that you can make in double amounts and plan to freeze the extra. Some nights your plan may say something as simple as cheese, bread and apples. Focus on your goal: you want to feed your family nourishing food that is less expensive than the food you fed them last month. Remember that your skills will increase and your expenses will decrease as you continue to focus on your goal. Don't try to do it all at once.

✦ **Homemade mixes.** Look in a basic cookbook for a cornbread, biscuit, pancake or muffin recipe. When you are making one of these for your family, set up five big Ziplocs along side your mixing bowl. Now, when it says to put a cup of flour in the bowl, also put a cup of flour in each of the bags. Continue doing this with all the dry ingredients in the recipe. (Do not put wet ingredients in the bag.) If your recipe calls for shortening, you can throw that in with the dry ingredients. When you have all the dry ingredients in the bowl and in the bags, stop and make a note on each bag, something like, "Muffin mix. Add 2 Tbsp. oil and 1 cup water. Bake at 425 degrees for 20 minutes." If you use instant milk and substitute soy flour for eggs (1 Tbsp. soy flour plus one Tbsp. water for each egg), there will be very little else to add when you use your mix.

✦ **Cook once, eat thrice.** Beans and rice, once cooked, are great convenience foods. Sometime when you are going to be home for a few hours, cook a big pot. Cooking beans doesn't really take much hands-on time if you are at home anyway. Pressure cookers are wonderful for cooking beans. If you don't have a pressure cooker, put the beans to soak in water in the morning. You'll be able to cook them in the evening in less time. Then make your menu plan so that you can use beans two or three times in the week to come. Rice, too, holds up well in the refrigerator. Use this principle with soups, refrigerator rolls, fried hamburger or TVP (see Resources for an explanation of TVP),and cooked grains that can be reheated in the microwave for breakfast.

✦ **Collect low-cost, easy recipes.** Every family's taste is different. When you find a low-cost, easy recipe that your family likes, make a copy and make a spot to keep them. It's impossible to keep everything in your head. Use your recipe collection for inspiration when you are planning the week's meals. For main dishes, don't forget burritos, stir-fry (to top the rice you've already cooked), soup, chili, "pizza" on french bread cut lengthwise and even scrambled eggs.

Here are a few recipes that have worked well for me and my thrifty friends:

LAYERED DINNER

In a casserole dish, layer sliced potatoes, chopped onions, ground beef or TVP, corn and a can of mushroom soup or a cup of white sauce. Bake at 350 degrees for an hour.

BEAN CASSEROLE

Mash or blend 2 cups pinto beans. Layer with flour tortillas and picante sauce (several layers). Top with enchilada sauce (optional) and cheese. Bake at 350 degrees until cheese melts.

QUICKIE SPAGHETTI SAUCE

For each 15-ounce can of tomato sauce, saute half of a medium onion and half a green bell pepper, chopped. Add onion and pepper to tomato sauce with a dash of garlic powder, a teaspoon of oregano and mushrooms if desired.

QUICKIE LASAGNE

1 package lasagne noodles
4 cups canned or homemade chunky spaghetti sauce
1 container ricotta cheese
1 pound white cheese

Put a thin layer of sauce in the bottom of a 9" x 12" pan. On uncooked lasagne noodles, spread a layer of ricotta cheese. Lay in pan, ricotta side up, and top with more sauce and grated cheese. Make another identical layer. Top with lasagne noodles, sauce and grated cheese. Cook at 350 degrees for one hour.

BARBEQUED BEANS AND VEGGIES

In a large pan, saute one medium onion and a half pound ground beef or TVP (optional). Add one bell pepper, chopped. Saute until onions are limp, then mix in one can or package of frozen corn and two cups beans (white, pinto, kidney and black beans all work) and ¾ cup barbeque sauce and cook until all ingredients are warm. Serve over rice or noodles.

CHEESE AND RICE DELIGHT

This dish actually looks like something that should be called "Glop", but it tastes delightful, hence its name. Mix 6 cups of cooked rice with 10 ounces of Monterey Jack or Mozzerella cheese, cubed. Add one small can chopped green chile peppers (if you chop these yourself, do NOT touch your eyes or your contact lenses). Add one 6 ounce carton plain yogurt and mix all ingredients together. Heat in oven or microwave until cheese is melted. Stir again to distribute cheese before serving.

INSTANT CREAM SAUCE FOR VEGETABLES

½ cup flour
½ cup dry milk (instant or non-instant)
2 Tbsp. onion granules or powder
2 tsp. salt
¼ tsp. pepper
½ cup butter

Mix all ingredients and cut in the butter until it is pea sized. To use, cook 2 cups of vegetables in ½ cup water. When they are done, stir in 4 Tbsp. of Instant Cream Sauce Mix and cook for a few minutes until thickened.

QUICKIE SCALLOPED POTATOES

Wash and slice 4 pounds of potatoes (peeling is optional). Put in a layer of potatoes and top with 1 Tbsp. chopped onion (or 1 Tbsp. onion granules), 1 Tbsp. flour, a sprinkle of salt and 1 Tbsp. butter (dotted across potatoes). Make three layers like this. Pour 2½ c. milk over it all. Bake covered at 350 degrees for 30 minutes, uncover and continue to cook for another 60 minutes.

MAGIC PIE

The magic part of this pie recipe is that a crust magically appears as it bakes. Like all pies, this can be made with fruit filling, or with quiche filling. Here's the fruit variety for a 10-inch pie pan:

4 cups fruit
¼ cup sugar
Spices (you choose)
¾ cup water
½ cup flour
1 tsp. baking powder
¼ tsp. salt
2 eggs
2 Tbsp. butter

Combine all ingredients except fruit in a blender. Stir in fruit and pour in greased pie pan. Bake 60 minutes at 325 degrees.

DUTCH BABIES

Mix in blender: three eggs, ¾ cup milk, and ¾ cup flour. Heat oven to 425 degrees. Put one-half stick of butter into a 9" x 12" pan and melt in oven. Pour in batter (on top of melted butter) and cook for 20 minutes. Top with fruit. This can be dessert or breakfast.

BANANA NUT CAKE (ONE PAN, NO BOWL)

When you have too-ripe bananas, throw them in the freezer, skin and all. Then when you want to bake with them, put them in the microwave for about one minute each. Remove and snip off the end of the banana. Squeeze the banana out of its skin, like toothpaste out of a tube. You'll barely have to mash them at all.

1½ cups flour
¾ cup sugar
1 tsp. baking powder
¼ tsp. baking soda
Dash salt
⅔ cup chopped nuts (optional)
2 mashed bananas
⅓ cup oil
⅓ cup milk
2 eggs

Heat oven to 350 degrees. Mix dry ingredients into an ungreased 8 or 9 inch baking pan. Stir with fork until well mixed. Blend in wet ingredients until smooth. Bake 30 - 35 minutes.

HOMEMADE ICE CREAM AND SORBETS

Ice cream is a favorite summer treat and an expensive one! Try these recipes for making your own. The following recipes can be frozen in an ice cream freezer, but to me it seems more convenient to use the still-freeze method (do this when you are going to be home for a few hours). To still-freeze, put your liquid ice cream in a freezer proof mixing bowl (it will freeze faster in a flat pan, but then you will have to transfer it to a mixing bowl). Leave it until a broad rim of ice forms around the edge - this can take from one to three hours depending on your freezer. At this point, take it out and whisk or beat with an electric mixer until smooth. Cover and return to the freezer. Repeat this process twice to give it a creamy, rather than icy, texture. You can freeze it in an airtight container for up to a week. If it's too hard when you take it out, leave it in the refrigerator during dinner or microwave it for 5 seconds.

VANILLA ICE CREAM

½ cup sugar
Dash salt
2 tsp. vanilla
3 cups, total, milk and whipping cream. Adjust the proportions for the fat content you want. More whipping cream equals more fat. More whipping cream also makes it taste more like premium ice cream. Add chopped fruit, chocolate chunks, etc. to vary the flavor. Freeze by either method.

FRUIT SORBET

2 cups fruit juice (lemon is a good flavor, too)
3 tsp. unflavored gelatin
½ cup sugar (¾ cup for lemon)
1 cup water

Mix sugar and gelatin in a saucepan. Add water, stir over low heat until sugar and gelatin are completely dissolved. Stir in fruit juice and freeze by either method.

MINTED TEA SORBET

2 cups mint tea, made with 5 tea bags or 3 Tbsp. loose leaves
⅓ cup sugar
1 cup water
2 Tbsp. lemon juice (optional)
Mix sugar into warm tea to dissolve. Let cool to room temperature. Add water and lemon juice. Freeze by either method.

Resources

• *The Tightwad Gazette* and *The Tightwad Gazette II*, Amy Dacyczyn, Random House, 1993 and 1995, $9.95 and $11.95. (The price book system is described in the first book.)

• A free booklet to get you started on organic gardening is available from Rodale Press, Circulation Department, 33 E. Minor Street, Emmaus, PA 18098. Ask for "The Basic Book of Organic Gardening."

• *Square Foot Gardening,* Mel Bartholomew, Rodale, 1981, $16.95. Also available from the publisher at (800)848-4735.

• *The Complete Book of Edible Landscaping,* Rosalind Creasy, Sierra Club Books, 1982, $22.00.

• *How to Grow More Vegetables*, John Jeavons, Ten Speed Press, 1995, $16.95. Also available from the publisher at (800)841-2665.

• TVP is textured vegetable protein. It is made entirely from soybeans and is available in the bulk section of natural foods grocery stores. When reconstituted (1 cup TVP with 7/8 cup hot water), it has the texture and appearance of ground beef, but it is approximately one quarter the cost of ground beef. (The weight of TVP when reconstituted is about 3 times heavier than when you buy it dry.) To give it more of a meat flavor, reconstitute it using hot water with soy sauce and smoke flavoring (sold next to the barbeque sauce) or with broth or bouillon. I saute it with onion granules to use in tacos. It works very well with tomato-based foods such as chili, spaghetti sauce, Sloppy Joes, etc. For lots of TVP recipes, get the TVP Cookbook by Dorothy Bates, The Book Publishing Company, (800)695-2241. Ask for their mail order catalog if you cannot find a local source of TVP.

When you compare the cost of buying ready made to cooking from scratch, you need to add in the cost of using your oven.

If you pay 8 cents per kilowatt hour for electricity: *
An electric oven on 350 degrees for one hour = 16 cents
A toaster oven on 425 degrees for one hour = 10 cents
An electric frying pan on 420 degrees for one hour = 7 cents
A crock pot on 200 degrees for one hour = 1 cent
A microwave on High for one hour = 12 cents

If you pay 60 cents per therm for gas: *
A gas oven at 350 degrees for one hour = 7 cents

* Your local utility company will tell you the price per kilowatt hour and per therm in your area.

HEALTH

We all want our children to be healthy. Health is so precious to us that we often spend hundreds of dollars attempting to bring it to our children. What I want to share with you in this chapter is my family's approach to dealing with health issues. I am not a medical professional and cannot prescribe or recommend health care, but I can share information with you and tell you what has worked for us.

✦ **Prevention.** OK, you've heard this a million times, but I'm going to bring it up again. Staying healthy is the best way to avoid medical costs and it is so much easier on little bodies and on the family's lifestyle. Set up situations where your kid get exercise, outside if you can. Make your home life tranquil and give kids a place to recharge to reduce their stress. Make sure that your small children are protected from things they might choke on, breakable objects, medicines and poisons, hot pans and electrical outlets. Give them bike helmets and make them wear their seat belts. Feed them good food. Role-play with them any potentially dangerous situations they might encounter on their own.

✦ **Do the cheap and easy things first.** If my child has trauma, like a broken arm, or a potentially life-threatening illness, I head for a health professional. Neither of those happen very often so the bulk of our health care efforts are directed at things like colds, allergies, and bumps and bruises. I am an advocate of natural medicine because there are many gentle treatments for children's common complaints that I have found to be effective. I will share these with you because most are not known by people unfamiliar with natural medicine. They are inexpensive, especially compared to anything I might get from a doctor, and I can just go get it myself without having a doctor recommend or prescribe it.

✦ **Drink water.** How much cheaper and easier can you get? Plain water has helped us with urinary tract infections, skin problems, coughs and colds. I just read about a study where 78% of the participants reported a reduction in their allergy symptoms just from drinking eight glasses of water a day. Water is absorbed into your body through your colon and flushes wastes, including toxins, out of the body through the kidneys.

A glass of warm salt water, gargled, makes a sore throat feel better.

✦ **Get enough sleep.** Sleep is the body's time to repair itself. I've found that when we've all had enough sleep, our quality of life is better overall - we're more alert, less grumpy and less likely to get sick. Getting enough sleep doesn't cost us anything. Make it a priority.

✦ **Boost your immune system.** There are stacks of articles being written about immune system function and things you can use to boost it. Not everybody agrees on what that is, but there are two things that have lots of literature pertaining to their beneficial effects: garlic and echinacea. Both are available at a natural foods store. Get a good brand of garlic capsules like Kyolic. Echinacea comes in capsule or tincture form. The tincture may be more potent, but it has a strong taste that my children object to, so I put it in their tea with honey or I give them the capsules with added goldenseal. My children very rarely have a cold that lasts for a week when they take garlic and echinacea. Two to three days is more common. Both are good for any kind of infection.

I also believe in Vitamin C, which is quite inexpensive, even from better companies. Vitamin C is cleared from the body in 12 hours, so it helps to give doses throughout the day. Please check the library for information on using Vitamin C, or just try it for yourself and see what you think. I do encourage you not to get grocery store brands of vitamins, which sometimes use fillers and binders that make it hard for the supplement to be absorbed. Low absorption equals money wasted.

Sugar decreases the immune response, so limit sugars when your little one is fighting off an illness. (So much for my theory that ice cream makes anything better.)

✦ **Breastfeed.** Breastfeeding has so many benefits over formula feeding in terms of health and money. Breastmilk has a powerful antimicrobial effect which helps protect infants from infection. Consequently, they have significantly fewer bouts of diarrhea, ear infections, respiratory infections and urinary tract infections. Studies have revealed a variety of benefits to older children who were breastfed, including less allergies, better vision, better intellectual attainment, and even indicate a protective factor against appendicitis, juvenile rheumatoid arthritis and multiple sclerosis. These studies are all on file at the La Leche League International office.

It's cheaper, too! A new study comparing the costs of formula feeding to breastfeeding for moms and babies enrolled in WIC and Medicaid programs revealed that breastfed babies had only *half* the pharmacology costs of formula-fed babies. That means parents of formula-fed babies were needing to buy twice as much medicine for their babies. This is a clear cash advantage to breastfeeding (beyond the savings on the cost of formula), not to mention the advantage of fewer agonizing nights up with a sick babe. See Resources at the end of this chapter for more information on this study.

Just to complete the litany of breastfeeding benefits, here's what it does for moms. Breastfeeding mothers lose twice as many pounds during baby's first year, have less breast cancer, better bone density and lower rates of ovarian cancer. They also have reduced gestational diabetes, less ulcerative colitis and less Crohn's disease. It's just hard to beat breastfeeding for health benefits to both moms and kids.

✦ **Arnica.** Arnica is an herb whose effect seems miraculous to me. If you rub it on a bump, it significantly reduces bruising. It works wonders on sprains and strained muscles. Buy a little jar of arnica salve or a tube of arnica gel at your natural foods store for about $5.00. Follow the instructions and do not apply it to places where the skin has been broken.

✦ **Oscillococcinum.** It took me a year just to learn to say this one, but you don't have to be able to say it to use it. This is a homeopathic preparation which was shown in a double-blind study to be a significantly more effective treatment of flu than the placebo. The instructions say to take it when you first get that flu feeling - aching in your bones and fever. Members of my family have had the first signs of flu four times this year and we took oscillococcinum and either did not get full-blown flu or only had it for one day (one of us). It costs about $4.00 for a three dose treatment from my food co-op. (See Resources to find it in your area.)

✦ **Homeopathics in general.** I believe homeopathics work. Some people in mainstream medicine believe they do not. I urge you to try it for yourself. A bottle of homeopathic remedy costs less than $5.00 (I get them from my food co-op for $3.00. My food co-op also has a kit of six remedies useful for children's illnesses for $10.00.) One area in which homeopathics are often used is earaches. In eleven years of using homeopathics, I have had one child on antibiotics for an ear infection one time. The rest of the time we have used one of two homeopathic remedies, Belladonna or Chamomilla, to get relief within hours. (See Resources for more written information about homeopathics.)

✦ **Herbs in general.** Get a good basic guide, such as *The Family Herbal* (see Resources), to help you use herbs. Some need to be used in limited doses (similar to when we use aspirin in limited doses). I have been very grateful to have herbs available when my child needed something to help her conquer her lingering cough or to boost her immune system. They are available from a natural foods store or food co-op.

✦ **Food for health.** A well-nourished child is much less likely to fall ill. When you are choosing food for your children, try to minimize the amount of saturated fats they get (like in burgers and fries) and maximize whole grains and fresh food.

We all have heard the ads from the Meat and Dairy Councils. While not advocating any particular lifestyle except a healthy one, I do want to share with you some numbers that the Meat and Dairy Councils will not give you in their ads. It is important to know the long term health effects of the food we feed our children now. In *The Nutrition*

Detective, Nan Fuchs states that a diet high in meat and/or soft drinks causes an excess of phosphorus in our bodies, which in turn prevents our bodies from using dietary calcium. This is important especially for our girl children, who need to start life with strong bones. The *South African Medical Journal* published a study which compared 75 lifelong vegetarians to a similar number of meat-eaters. Over their lives, the vegetarians spent an average of 139 days in the hospital - the meat-eaters spent 654. EarthSave's *Realities for the 90's* gives the following data: Risk of death from heart attack for the average American man - 50%. Risk of death from heart attack for a man who consumes no meat - 15%. Risk of death from heart attack for a man who consumes no meat, dairy products or eggs - 4%. Whew! No matter how you feel about eating meat, these numbers are impressive. It's clear that cutting down on your family's meat consumption increases their long term health.

As thrifty parents, we also want the most nutrition for our dollar. Remember that empty calories are not a good buy, health-wise. Food and health are so intertwined. Fortunately for us, as we cook more from scratch and from our gardens in order to save money, we are also easily increasing the amount of nourishment that our children's food provides for them.

When You Do Need To See The Doctor

Make a list of questions you want to ask the doctor so that you won't forget any in the office. If the doctor prescribes a medication, ask if there is a generic equivalent and if they have samples (drug companies pass out free samples to doctors). Pharmacists have written information about each drug that they will give you if you ask for it. Other places to find out about a drug are *The Physician's Desk Reference (The PDR)* or *The New People's Pharmacy* by Joe Graedon.

If you do not have health insurance that covers the doctor visit, ask the doctor's staff if there is a discount for cash payments. Doctors will sometimes make adjustments in the fee schedule. For example, when my dermatologist learned that my health insurance didn't cover office visits, he didn't charge me  for the lab work which was done within their office.

Sometimes you can just call the doctor's office with a question or two and skip the visit and the bill for the visit. Don't abuse this priviledge, but do remember that you are paying your doctor to be your expert advisor. He or she is working for you and should not mind spending a minute or two on something that can be handled by phone. A helpful book is *Getting the Best From Your Doctor* by Wesley Smith and Ralph Nader. (See Resources at the end of this chapter.)

If Your Child Needs Hospitalization

Having a child in the hospital is hard enough, without the trauma of deciphering a hospital bill. Still, attention to the bill can save you money. This is true even if you were only in the emergency room to have a cut stitched.

If your doctor is affiliated with more than one hospital and your child is having a non-emergency procedure, shop around. Compare the prices of rooms at different hospitals and check with the billing office to see if costs are reduced if you provide your own linen, nightgowns and meals.

Health Insurance

There is a large portion of America's workers who do not have health insurance provided by their employers. If you are one of these workers, check to see if there is any professional organization or other group through which you might get group insurance. It is less expensive than buying it individually.

My husband and I are self-employed and I spent several months shopping around for health insurance that fit within our budget. We have opted for a policy for major medical only, with a $5,000 deductible. We chose this policy because it was less than $100/month, one third the cost of any policy that paid for every prescription and doctor's visit. We visit the doctor's office infrequently and therefore wouldn't have often used the office visits portion of the more expensive policy. This policy assures us that a major illness or accident isn't going to make us bankrupt - we can handle the $5,000 deductible somehow, it is the $50,000 or $100,000 potential hospital bill that would undo us financially. My policy is from American Republic (see Resources). Other companies are apparently offering this type of policy now.

Go to the library and look at the *Best's Insurance Reports* for any company from which you are thinking of buying insurance. Use only those companies with high ratings. For $15, you can get a list of policies that meet the price and coverage guidelines you specify from Quotesmith, (800)556-9393. This is a way to ferret out policies you may not already be aware of and quickly compare prices. You can also get this information online from the Insurance News Network <http://www.insure.com>.

HMOs

"Managed care", as HMOs are called, is offered by many employers. When choosing an HMO, the *Harvard Health Letter* points out that you should look for wellness programs, routine screeening, chronic disease management, psycho-therapy services and rehabilitation programs. Talk with others who are using the HMO you are considering and ask them pointed questions about the level of care they have received before you make your choice.

Resources

• *Getting the Best From Your Doctor,* Wesley Smith and Ralph Nader, CSRL Books, Box 19367, Washington, DC 20036, $10 (postage paid).

• *Everybody's Guide to Homeopathic Medicines*, Stephen Cummings and Dana Ullman, J.P. Tarcher, 1991, $10.95.

• *Homeopathic Remedies for Children,* Speight, Atrium Publishing, 1995, $8.95.

• Oscillococcinum is available from natural foods stores. It is made by Boiron. Call them at (800)264-7661 to find out where it is carried in your area.

• *Vaccines: Are They Really Safe and Effective?*, Neil Miller, New Atlantean Press, 1992, $8.95. Available at bookstores or from the publisher at The New Atlantean Press, P.O. Box 9638, Santa Fe, NM 87504.

• *The Family Herbal: A Guide to Natural Health Care for Yourself and Your Children*, Barbara and Peter Theiss, Healing Arts Press, 1993, $16.95.

• *The Womanly Art of Breastfeeding*, La Leche League International. Call (800)525-3243 for the free La Leche League book catalog, which includes many books to help mothers who are breastfeeding.

•The Economic Benefit of Breastfeeding. Debbie Montgomery and Patricia Splett. *Breastfeeding Update* 1996; 4:1-2. For more information on this study, contact Debbie Montgomery at the Colorado Department of Health, 4300 Cherry Creek Drive South, Denver, CO 80222.

• RPS discount mail order pharmacy. A source of prescription drugs that may be lower than your local drugstore. Call them to compare prices. (800)456-2277.

• *How to Find the Best Doctors, Hospitals, and HMOs for You and Your Family: Pocket Guide,* Castle Connolly Medical Ltd., 1995, $9.95.

• American Republic Insurance. (800)247-2190. This is the health insurance company I am currently using for a low-cost, high deductible policy. Call for rates.

• Insurance News Network. Listing of Standard and Poor's ratings of insurance carriers. <http://www.insure.com>

HOW ONE FAMILY MAKES IT HAPPEN

Linda Prince has four daughters, who range in age from 4 to 22. When she found herself a single mother, she had to learn quickly how to be frugal just so she and her family could survive. Now remarried, and with her own home-based business in Montana, Linda recalls the things she learned which enabled her family to thrive, no matter what their income. "I learned to keep things simple," she says, "for instance, babies really only need warmth, shelter, breastmilk and diapers. I learned to say, 'This is what we do in *our* family.' I learned that if I gave the kids a 'cooling off' period when they wanted me to buy something, sometimes the purchase became less important." Linda's oldest daughter is now working her way through college, using many of the frugality skills she learned from her mom.

TRAVEL

Is bargain travel really possible with kids? We all know you can get great deals if you are a single adult and can leave at a moment's notice, but what about those of us who want to go as a family? The AAA Travel Service Report for 1994 states that the average cost of lodging and meals for a family of four was $188 a day! With planning, and no matter what your situation, you *can* significantly reduce the dollars you spend on travel, certainly below this national average.

The details of getting ready to travel can be very overwhelming! Try to stay focused on the big reason you are travelling: fun, relaxation, reconnecting with loved ones. Those goals can be accomplished in an assortment of settings. Your job is to create a setting that will not overtax your financial resources.

Travel By Car

Car travel is usually the least expensive way to go. However, long car trips with children have other costs: stress, restaurants, goodies we buy them to keep them busy. Here are some ideas thrifty families use to reduce those costs.

✦ **Toys.** Go by the thrift store and get several 10 cent toys and scan their offerings on books, games and puzzles for ones which could be used in a car (or stock up on these during yard sale season). My local Goodwill store has bags of about 20 little toys for $2.00.

✦ **Art supplies.** Take along some crayons (empty baby wipe containers are good for holding crayons in the car) and paper or coloring books.

✦ **Tapes.** Find some new story tapes and kids' music tapes at the library or borrow some from friends. This can be a lifesaver for that last hour in the car.

✦ **Food art.** Get a plastic bag for each child and fill it with little marshmallows, raisins, O's cereal and toothpicks. They can use these materials to concoct odd edible inventions. Don't give this to kids who are still at choking age or who need supervision with toothpicks.

✦ **Car rental.** If you must rent a car, consider Rent-A-Wreck, Rent-A-Dent or Ugly Duckling. We have had good luck doing this. While the names bring up images of rusted fenders tied on with baling wire, the cars we've had are nothing like that. In fact, I've sometimes had to look hard to find anything wrong with them. The cost is considerably less than a regular

car rental agency. If you plan to rent any car, check with your car insurance agent and with your credit card company to see if you may already be covered in rental cars. If you are, don't buy the rental agency's insurance (although they may use scare tactics to try to get you to). Also, check to see if they have child car seats and if they charge extra for them. You may want to take your own car seat along if they do.

✦ **Picnic.** Take food like cheese, fruit and sandwiches and your own canned drinks (or cups with lids) to use for one meal a day.

✦ **Stretch your legs.** Stop at a city park and let the kids run around for an hour. Even little towns often have nice parks.

✦ **Games.** See Resources at the end of this chapter for books full of travel games - look for them at your library.

✦ **To avoid.** Try not to make pit stops at souvenir palaces. Even kids who understand that their parents are not going to buy this stuff, want to look at it anyway. I find that it takes a massive amount of energy to get in and out of places like that.

Consider giving your children a vacation allowance - a set amount of money they can spend during the trip. This tactic really cuts down on the "Mom, will you buy me this?" syndrome, while teaching them about budgeting in a scaled down form.

Travel By Airplane

There are times when you may choose to fly. I'm inserting a word of caution here. Jetting off for a week in Paradise can easily eat up thousands of dollars. If you are looking for ways to minimize spending, really weigh the amount of fun and relaxation you will be getting for the amount of money you'll be forking over. That said, if you do decide to fly, there are several ways to lower the fares.

◆ **Kids for free.** On most domestic flights, kids under two fly for free. If the plane is fully booked, you must hold this child in your lap. Each child that is flying free must be accompanied by an adult, so if you, Mom, are taking your 6-month old and your 18-month-old by yourself to visit your relatives, you will have to find another adult on the flight who is willing to officially "accompany" your second child. Get to check-in early and look in the line for a likely person. You might end up with two kids on your lap if the flight is full, so if you are doing this, try not to fly at peak times. Although you can't reserve a seat for your baby, when you are making your own seat arrangements, ask for the seat next to you to be "blocked". This means it will be one of the last to be filled. Children flying under this arrangement usually have no checked luggage allowance. Ask the airline about the adult luggage limits (usually two or three bags under a certain size).

If you are running short on packing space, remember that you can have a carry-on bag, *plus* a purse (of any size), a diaper bag, reading material and you can wear clothing with things stuffed in the pockets.

◆ **Low fare travel agent.** Travel agencies receive a percentage of the dollar amount they sell. Getting you a lower price fare gets them a lower commission, so trusting your travel agent to tell you about the lowest fare can be hazardous to your pocketbook. One agency that I know of that has built its business specializing in low fares is Associated Travel, 600 Anton Blvd., Suite B, Costa Mesa, CA 92626. (714) 545-3335 (Once you become a client, they give you an 800 number to call.) You can pay by credit card and they will mail you the tickets.

◆ **Online information.** Computer networks can offer a whole range of travel information. America Online lists travel deals in their "Traveler's Corner". Through Compuserve,

America Online, Prodigy and GEnie, you can get in to the Eaasy Sabre system which lists all flights and their prices. By using the Bargain option, you can even find the lowest fare.

✦ **Fare rebates.** If your fare is over $300 and you have worked out your own itinerary (that is, you require no planning help), Travel Avenue will rebate to you half their commission, or approximately 8%. You can even go ahead and make the reservation with the airline yourself, but you must call Travel Avenue the same day you make the reservation to get this deal. Their number is (800)333-3335.

✦ **Tips on air travel with children.** According to George Albert Brown, author of *The Airline Passenger's Guerilla Handbook*, small extras are available from most airlines. Brown, who has traveled with his own children, mentions free spare diapers on the plane, bassinets (order in advance), entertainment kits, children's meals and snacks and drinks upon request. He notes that although airlines request that you check your stroller with your baggage, you can actually take it to the gate and they will store it in the cabin or check it there into the baggage hold. Brown's book is chock full of information for air travelers. Look for it in Resources. Take advantage of the preboarding offered to people traveling with small children. When you hear the call for preboarding, you march to the head of the boarding line and on to the airplane. If you've had the foresight to reserve the bulkhead seats, you'll have more room and be closer to the bathrooms.

For a free pamphlet "Kids and Teens in Flight", write to the Office of Consumer Affairs, Room 10405, U.S. Department of Transportation, 400 Seventh Street SW, Washington, DC, 20590. Many of the entertainment ideas in the car travel section above are appropriate to air travel.

Travel By Train

Air and train fares change all the time, so you'll have to compare to see which is less expensive. Train travel is, hands down, the most fun. There are no seat belts, lots of room to move around and sights to see. The trains themselves and their conductors harken back to an earlier era, which is fascinating to children. However, from my personal experience, I urge you not to take trains during holiday seasons. To get information on fares or package deals, call Amtrak at (800)872-7245. They do offer free coloring books and balloons upon request and the dining car has a kids' menu, although bringing your own food on board is quite easy and is commonly done. Some trains also show morning cartoons in the lounge car.

Lodging

One of the big expenses of family travel, lodging is also the one with the most options. Motels, of course, are the most common, but alternatives abound.

✦ **Hostels.** The image of hostels is one of college students with backpacks. Actually, people of all ages, including families with children, are welcome to stay at hostels. While most are set up dorm-style, with men in one room and women in another, Hostelling International says that many hostels have private rooms available for families. Guests must bring or rent sheets, pillowcases and towels and must clean up after themselves. Additionally, you can only use the space during the hours between the evening check-in time and the morning check-out time. In exchange, members get rates that are substantially lower than motel rates, use of the kitchen and discounts to area attractions and restaurants. I called the hostel in Santa Fe, New Mexico to compare its rate to that of local motels, where the mean rate for a family of four (outside of the downtown area) is $75/night and the Motel 6 rate is $49/night. At the hostel, the rate for two adult members is $24/night for dorm space (kids under 12 stay free), $48 for a private room with bath, and $40 for a private room with a bath shared with one other room.

THERE ARE TWO HOSTEL ASSOCIATIONS:

- Hostelling International - American Youth Hostels
733 15th Street, NW
P.O. Box 37613
Washington, DC 20013
(202) 783-6161

Family rate to join - $35. Average rate per adult per night for dorm accomodations - $17.

- American Association of International Hostels
250 West 77th St., Suite 906
New York, NY 10024
(212) 769-9039

They sell individual memberships only for $5 each, so a family of four would be $20. The membership entitles each member to a $1 per night reduction in rate at the hostel. Rate per adult per night for dorm accomodations $10-$18.

✦ **University student rooms.** Rooms and apartments which usually house students are open to the public during vacation periods, and usually include access to the university facilities and the dining room. To compare to the Santa Fe prices

noted in the hostel section, above, I called the College of Santa Fe, which does provide lodging. Rooms with two single beds occupied by two adults are $36 per night, $30 if you bring your own linen. If your children are still small enough to sleep with you, or if you could make them a bed on the floor, they can stay free. If they need their own room, they pay full price. The rooms have sinks. Shared bathrooms are down the hall.

✦ **Home exchange programs.** Basically, home exchange means just that. You let another family stay in your house and they let you stay in theirs. Several exchange services exist to hook up families seeking exchanges. HomeLink USA, which claims to be "America's oldest and largest home exchange organization", charges $79 to join and sends out a quarterly directory. They have listings both in the USA and overseas, mostly in Europe. If you plan to be in one place for a week or more and live in an area frequented by tourists, this option could be worth investigating. (HomeLink's number is (800)638-3841.)

For a more complete listing of home exchange services, university student rooms and hostels, as well as YMCA's, Bed and Breakfasts and economy and mid-price hotels and motels, look for the *Budget Lodging Guide.* This 500-page directory is useful for finding low-cost lodging in the particular areas you will be visiting. (See Resources at the end of this chapter.)

✦ **Hotels and Motels.** Although national hotel chains have 800 reservation numbers, experts say that you will almost always get a better deal if you call the individual hotel in which you are thinking of staying. If you are staying during the week, motels will sometimes give you a business discount if you ask for it and give them your business card when you check in. Also ask if breakfast or happy hour comes free with the room. If for some reason you don't want to eat the free breakfast, you can always save it in a doggie bag for later.

If your family requires two adjoining rooms, book one adult into each room. Each adult will be charged a single rate, since kids often stay free when staying with an adult.

All The Other Little Things

✦ **Traveler's checks.** Some banks offer free traveler's checks, but most don't. If you have a AAA membership, you can get free traveler's checks through them. (The $64/ year also covers emergency road service, tour books and trip accidents reimbursement up to $300. See Resources for AAA's address.) You can conceivably use a credit card for most purchases and cash for everything else. Of course, this will only work if you keep up with how much you are spending and pay off the credit card when you get home. Ask your bank if your ATM card can be used in machines across the country. By getting cash out at intervals, you can avoid carrying large sums of cash, but will have to pay an ATM fee. Compare your total traveler's check vs. ATM fees to see which is the least expensive choice for you.

✦ **Area information.** Call the 800 operator to see if there are 800 numbers for state or city information in the areas you will be visiting. A letter to the Chamber of Commerce in any town will usually get you lots of information about that town and the surrounding area. Libraries often have books which list numbers for information about states, cities and attractions. (One such book is the *Guide to Free Attractions* by Don and Pam Wright. Unfortunately, this book is out of print and somewhat out of date, but it can provide a starting point if your library has it.)

 ✦ **Camping.** Camping is one of the best kind of vacations families can take. It's inexpensive, and once you get set up, it's relaxing. Plus, it is not consumer oriented - what is there to buy out in nature? A camping vacation offers a kind of closeness and deep relaxation that is often missing when our every minute is scheduled with activities and sights to see.

Resources

• *The Airline Passenger's Guerilla Handbook*, George Albert Brown, The Blakes Publishing Group, 1989, $14.95.

• *Guide to Free Campgrounds,* and *Camping on a Shoestring*, Don Wright, Cottage Publications, (800)272-5518, $14.95 each.

• *Camping With Kids*, Don Wright, Cottage Publications, (800)272-5518, $9.95.

• The *Let's Go* series. Look for this series at your bookstore. *Let's Go* publishes guides to individual cities inside the U.S. and countries outside the U.S. that includes many money saving tips. They try to make their guides helpful to families as well as single travelers.

• *On the Road: Fun Travel Games and Activities*, George Shea, Sterling, 1992, $5.95.

• *Travel Games for the Family*, Marie Boatness, Canyon Creek Press, 1993, $6.95.

• *Frommer's Budget Travel* series and *Frommer's Great Travel Value* series. Travel guides geared to travelers seeking low prices.

• American Automobile Association (AAA). Call (800)765-0766 and ask for the 800# of the club in your area.

HOLIDAYS

What is it about holidays that makes childrens' hearts sing? The anticipation of presents and candy undoubtably does have something to do with it, but what really makes holidays extra special are the family traditions and meanings that we attach to them. Children love traditions, especially those in which they participate. A box full of valentines and a bag of chocolate kisses is fun. Making visible the love we have for our friends and family is satisfying to our souls. The valentines and candy without the family conversation about making love visible is a one-dimensional celebration, and children definitely know it. After they open the cards and eat the candy, they want more or they whine about something, really meaning, "Is that all there is?" They want the soul satisfaction.

Fortunately, the things which make holidays satisfying to children don't cost anything. Most you couldn't even buy if you wanted to. These are your family times together when you, as parent, have an unparalled opportunity to "create family". If you don't already have traditions, make some. Identify what each holiday means to you and share that with your children. It's easy to let this part go in the hub-bub of holiday preparation, but I can't emphasize enough how important it is for your children. A beneficial side effect for you is that it decreases the focus on material goods.

The Winter Holidays

It is hard to enjoy holidays, especially Christmas, when we are stressed out. Identify the most important parts of the celebration to you and let the rest go. Read *Unplug the Christmas Machine* and talk to your family and friends about the vision you have for a more relaxed holiday.

However, gift giving will probably always have some part in your holidays, as will decor, parties, special food and all the other dozens of little ways we spend our money during holiday times. Look ahead to find many ways to reduce those costs for each holiday.

Ornaments

✦ **Cinnamon-Applesauce Ornaments.** These are not edible, but they smell great.

Mix ¾ cup applesauce and one package unflavored gelatin in small saucepan and let stand 3 minutes. Heat over medium heat, stirring constantly until it simmers. In a bowl, mix 6 Tbsp. cinammon, 3 Tbsp. ground cloves (buy spices in bulk at your natural foods market), and ¼ cup cornstarch. Stir in the applesauce mixure. Turn out and knead for 30 seconds. Use dough within 30 minutes. Keep portion you are not working with in plastic. Roll dough between sheets of plastic to ¼-inch thickness. Cut out ornaments with cookie cutters. Use a straw to make a hole for hanging. Dry on wire rack overnight. Makes about 24 2-inch ornaments.

✦ **Pinecones** with M&M's glued here and there in the spaces between their "petals" is festive.

✦ **Make felt animals** using a cookie cutter for a pattern. Each animal needs two sides. Sew them together with embroidery thread in a blanket stitch and stuff them with anything. Cotton balls work well for stuffing.

✦ **Use the salt dough** recipe under Art Materials in the Entertainment and Education chapter. Make an outline of each child's hand in salt dough. Remember to add a hole for hanging. These can be pretty heavy with big hands. When owners of those little hands grow up, looking at the ornaments can warm a mother's heart.

✦ **Go through** your child's little toys to find ones that could be hung on the tree.

✦ **For a country look,** cut out strips of fabric with pinking shears and use as ribbons to tie on the branches.

✦ **For ready-made ornaments,** hit the after Christmas sales. Simply buying one or two ornaments a year during this time can quickly add up to a collection. They should be at least 50% off. If you find a store with a large inventory, go back or call at one or two week intervals to find out if they have marked them down further. There's a big hobby store in my area where things eventually reach 90% off. I also buy my wrapping paper and ribbon then, too.

✦ **Look in the library** for many, many ideas. Gather up the ideas that use what you have or can come by very inexpensively.

Christmas Decor

✦ **Let your little ones** paint a scene with tempera paint on the inside of your patio door. Of course, put down newspapers and wear paint smocks. After the holidays, it easily washes off with soap and water. This, in itself, can be a fun activity for your small children.

✦ **Candles.** We often use candles to symbolize light. Many winter holidays include the use of candles and can be acquired at yard sales throughout the year, after-holiday sales, or made at home. Christmas colors are green and red, Hanukkah's blue and white and Kwanzaa's red, black and green.

✦ **Creches.** Children love the nativity scene. Help your children to make a simple one of clothespin people. Wooden clothespins and the bases that hold them upright can be

purchases at the hobby store. Dress them in felt. The animals can be basic construction paper, folded in half (see illustration).

✦ **Window ornaments.** Save your tissue paper throughout the year (wrinkled is OK). Cut it up into one inch squares and have the kids glue it onto a 12-inch piece of wax paper, so that the pieces cover the whole surface of the wax paper, one layer thick. Outline a big star on dark, solid colored paper no larger than 12 inches square. You'll need two stars for each window ornament you make. Now trim away all but the outside inch on both stars, leaving a "frame". Put another piece of wax paper over your child's tissue paper collage, sandwiching the tissue paper inside the two pieces of wax paper. Now sandwich the entire wax paper assembly between your two star frames. Trim the excess wax paper and tissue paper from around the outside of the star and glue the edges securely together. This looks quite pretty with the sun shining through it. People repeatedly commented on ours.

✦ **Paper dolls** that unfold into a long garland are beloved of children. Any shape can be used, as long as there are two points on each side left  connected. Fold a length of paper like you would a fan, leaving enough room on each fold for your design. Cookie cutters are good patterns for this. Also, look in children's books for basic shapes to trace, or draw your own.

✦ **Take the kids out** into nature and see what you can find. Gather a big basket of pinecones to put by your front door. Tie a ribbon on it. If you're feeling like taking on a larger project, gather wreath makings. Get sprigs of evergreen for the kids to tuck over your mirrors and pictures. Sand dollars, dried starfish and many shells make beautiful tree ornaments.

✦ **Again, go see** what the library has to offer you. Sort through for those many ideas that can be put together for a pittance.

Food

During the winter holidays, most of us feel the urge to do some baking. If you are working to lower your food bill, you may have already incorporated baking into your life. Truly, baking is not any harder or more time consuming than going to the mall at holiday time. It does take more time if you let the children help, but then it provides them with a fun activity where they are learning a useful life skill and you are making memories.

I find the holidays a tempting time to buy expensive ingredients to make "special" recipes. If I think about it and look in my cookbooks, I can always find something just as good that doesn't use those expensive ingredients. Putting more energy into the presentation can make it feel special. For instance, mashed potatoes can be piped from a pastry bag for a "fancy" dinner. Meals can be served in courses. This kind of cooking does take more time, but it needn't take more money. Make the table look good. Use the napkins you got at 75% off last year or collect red and green fabric when you see it at yard sales and stitch up some cloth napkins. Let the kids make place cards. Light candles. Ordinary food suddenly looks better in this setting!

Inexpensive Gifts Kids Can Give

✦ **Grow narcissus.** Narcissus bulbs are sold in nurseries during the fall for about 65¢ per bulb. Put three of these in a 50¢ thrift store bowl or plastic-lined basket. Add enough gravel to anchor the bulbs in place. (Look for sources of free gravel. Think of it as little rocks and get your kids to help you spot some. You don't need much.) Keep the bowl filled with water up to the bottom of the bulbs. Put in a spot with some light. In about five weeks, you'll have flowers beginning to open. To use this as a Christmas present, it needs to be started right after Thanksgiving.

✦ **Bread dough shapes.** Any basic yeast dough can be made into cute shapes such as teddy bears, wreaths or candy canes. Add a red ribbon accent and wrap in plastic wrap.

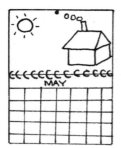

✦ **Calendars.** Save your children's artwork throughout the year. Let them pick 12 drawings that are 8½" x 11", or that can be cropped to that size. Make a calendar master by marking squares for the days - seven squares across and five down. Be sure to leave a place for the name of the month, but do not put in the numbers or month. (After the calendar is made have your children write the dates and month in by hand.) Have this master copied 12 times onto card stock (about $1.20). While at the copy store, assemble the calendar with the artwork for January facing the first calendar page, then the artwork for February facing the second calendar page and so on. Have the copy store bind this with a spiral binder. My local copy shop, part of a national chain, does this for $1.95. Voila! A beautiful gift for the grandparents for under $3.50! The kids may get requests for a new one every year.

✦ **Earring holder.** This project, is quick, fun and cheap. Buy a wooden frame at a yard sale. Let your child paint it or decorate it in any way. Trim a piece of plastic needlepoint canvas (less than 50¢ for an 8½" x 11" piece from the hobby store) to fit in the frame's opening and tack it to the back if needed. Give it to someone to use as a great storage area for pierced earrings.

✦ **Totebags, pillowcases, aprons, potholders.** Provide your child with "blanks" of any of these items and fabric paint or fabric crayons with which to decorate them. All of these items are easy and quick to sew, or get them at the hobby store when they are on sale. Decorating "blanks" is so popular with crafters now that most hobby stores have a whole section of them. Fabric crayons are an inexpensive and mess-free way to decorate permanently. Look for a package of eight crayons. It will include instructions on how to set the color so that it can be washed. If you already have a supply of fabric paint, you can let the children use it with supervision. One year I made denim (old blue jeans) potholders and used a tracing of each child's hand as a pattern for fabric paint decor. Then I wrote each child's name and age below her hand. I even made tracings of some of the kids' friends hands and gave potholders to their parents as a surprise. When I go to those homes now, I still see those potholders being used or saved as a memento of childhood.

✦ **Potpourri.** Save your dried flower petals throughout the year. If you don't have your own flower garden, ask a gardener to save them for you when they "deadhead" their flowers. Cut flowers from the florist can still be dried after they wilt. Spread them out in a single layer and leave them until they are dry. It's OK if they are shriveled. When they are completely dry, put in a paper bag. By Christmas, you should have a good amount. When oranges are in season, save the peels the same way and break them into small pieces. To make potpourri, mix your flower petals and orange peels with cinnamon sticks (buy them in bulk from the herb section of a natural foods grocery), ground cinnamon and little pine cones or acorns. If you want a vanilla smell, leave out the cinnamon and add a piece of paper soaked in vanilla that you have torn up into tiny pieces. You can use the soaked paper method with any essential oil, or sprinkle a few drops right on the potpourri and stir. This is an easy kid project.

To make a bag for your potpourri, cut a rectangle that is three times as long as it is wide. Fold it in half, sew up the sides and trim the top with pinking shears, or hem. Fill it about two thirds full of potpourri and tie it closed with a ribbon, If you are making cinnamon potpourri, you can tie on one of your cinnamon/applesauce ornaments (see above). This makes a very inexpensive hostess gift, gift for the neighbors or for your kids' teachers.

✦ **Pressed flower pictures.** Here's another use for summer blooms. Collect several small (1" or less) blossoms and put them between two pieces of wax paper in a big book that you're not going to be using for a few weeks. If you want to have a book just for pressing flowers, buy a heavy tome at a yard sale, save phone books from big cities or save the Penney's catalog. When they are completely dry, let your children arrange them into a pleasing picture. Glue them in place by lifting each bloom gently and placing a tiny dot of glue underneath. By using yard sale frames and even just mat boards, your children can have a very finished gift to give. Wildflowers and some grasses work well in these pictures.

✦ **Beaded necklaces and bracelets.** When you go to yard sales, look for old costume jewelry and jars of beads that can be had for a quarter. Snip the strings and put the beads out in Ziploc bags or bowls and let your child string beads to his or her heart's content. Clasps for the necklaces can be purchased in the jewelry findings department of a hobby store and should be tied *firmly* to the necklace string. You can also buy the string for necklaces at the hobby store or you can use dental floss. I like to use elastic thread because it works well for bracelets, too, and doesn't require a clasp. At my hobby store, plastic beads in Christmas shapes are always available in the after Christmas sales. These make bracelets that are fun for one kid to give another at Christmas the next year.

Valentine's Day

I'm a big fan of Valentine's Day, especially since it has become a day to send loving thoughts to all our friends and family, as well as to those with whom we have a romance. The little valentines made for children to give one another are very inexpensive. To create nicer, more personalized valentines for pennies, gather together a valentine making kit. Here's some possible kit ingredients:

- Heavy white and red paper
- All weights of white, red and pink paper
- Doilies
- Stickers
- Pictures cut from magazines or saved from cards that have been given to you
- A heart-shaped hole punch
- Rubber stamps

- Pages from seed catalogs of flowers in bloom, cut into heart shapes with pinking shears
- Ribbon snippets
- Pressed flowers

The way to make this kit for pennies is to collect things for it throughout the year. Save wrapping paper, cards or anything else that comes to you that you don't want to keep forever, but seem too pretty to throw away. One of my favorite little scenes was part of the packaging for an iron-on  applique! When your child brings home a flyer printed on red or pink paper, throw it in your kit. When you go to the printer to get your free scrap paper, use some of the nice heavy papers you get for your kit. When you are at yard sales, snap up the half-used package of doilies for ten cents and grab that stack of nice, but odd sized envelopes that nobody else seems to want. While you're there, look for stickers, bottles of glitter, and sequins. Anything that's metallic and sparkly is appealing to children. Save Christmas wrapping paper and candy wrappers that are gold or shiny. Look in the Entertainment and Education Chapter under Art to find out how to acquire rubber stamps for less. My kit has taken a few years to become "complete". I asked for the heart hole punch as a birthday present one year and I find that I use it the year round.

About two weeks before Valentine's Day, make a time for your family to sit around the dining room table making valentines. My mother-in-law was here this year during our valentine making session and had more fun than any of us! In years past, I have taken my kit and rubber stamp collection to a friend's house. She's one of my cohorts in thrift and in crafts, so she also had her own kit. We spread everything out over the table and both families spent the afternoon playing and making valentines.

My friend Linda takes this one step further. She has a valentine making party and invites all the children in the neighborhood. She serves pink tea and punch, and pink pudding.

Quick and Easy Valentine Gifts

✦ **Wrap a kiss.** Put on red lipstick and make a lip imprint on a piece of paper. Your boys may not want to do this, but if you, like me, have all girls, everyone can make an imprint and then you can frame it and give it to Dad.

✦ **Chocolate is good.** Bake up a heart-shaped cake. Divide the batter between a square cake pan and a round cake pan. When baked, cut the round cake in half, so that you have two half circles. Fit each half circle to one side of the square and top with frosting.

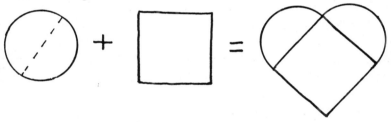

✦ **An easy necklace.** At the hobby or bead store, buy a heart shaped bead (under $1.00). String it on satin cording.

✦ **Make an impression.** Give heart-shaped rubber stamps that you got at last year's after-Valentine's Day sale.

✦ **Cups and candy.** Heart motif mugs are on sale after Valentine's Day, too, and can make a nice gift with a bag of something sweet tucked inside. One year for Valentine's Day gifts for my daughters, I got "I'm So Glad You're My Daughter" and "Best Kid Ever" mugs at the thrift store for 75¢ each and filled them with candy and a little doll I made for each girl. They ask for warm drinks in "their" mugs all winter.

✦ **Flowers on the cheap.** Forced bulbs are a perfect gift for this winter holiday. This is a plan-ahead gift, because you must buy the bulbs in the fall. Narcissus and hyacinths both work well because they can be grown in water. They take five or six weeks to bloom, so start them right after New Year's. Narcissus can be grown in pretty thrift store bowls or plastic lined baskets, with the bulbs anchored with small rocks. Hyacinths need a "hyacinth glass". Although you can buy these specifically for hyacinths, a lower cost alternative is to get a thrift store vase shaped like the bottom of an hour glass. The idea is that the neck must be small enough to support the bulb without letting it slip through into the water below. Put your bulb in its glass and fill it up so that the bottom touches water. When it blooms, tie a bow around the neck of the vase and take it to some lucky recipient. Bulbs are about 65¢ apiece and vases can be had for 75¢ or less.

Keep bow makings handy by buying a roll of ribbon when it is on sale at the hobby store. Gold goes with everything. If you are using new ribbon, a length that will tie around a vase will probably cost you around 50¢. Total cost for hyacinth: $1.90.

✦ **I love you because . . .** Fill up a jar with multicolored slips of paper on which you've written things that you appreciate about the person to whom you are giving the gift. This is a good one for kids to make for a parent. Have them remember specific times that the person did something that helped them or made them laugh.

The Spring Holidays

During this season of renewal, we like to surround ourselves with images of nature. Take advantage of nature's bounty to decorate your home. Cut a few stems from flowering bushes and put them in vases inside. Find an appropriate branch and create an Easter tree. Anchor it with rocks in an empty flower pot. When you make scrambled eggs, keep the shells intact by blowing the egg part into a bowl. When rinsed, these can be dyed or decorated just like boiled eggs, except these can be hung on your tree. Look through your children's little toys to find any little Easter-like thing that is light enough to be hung on the tree. Let the kids make drawings to hang there. Glue together a tiny nest of twigs and add clay eggs.

Although Easter has become fairly commercial, you don't need to spend much money to celebrate it. Dwell on the religious or spiritual meaning of the season. Many religions have a major celebration in the spring and they all seem to share the theme of new life springing forth.

In America, most families have Easter baskets for their children on Easter morning. It's easy to spend $20.00 per child just filling an Easter basket! Substitute a few of these for more expensive choices:

✦ **Tiny flower pots** (about 39 cents at the nursery). If you like, add a few marigold seeds in a miniscule envelope you make.

✦ **Fluffy rabbits.** Cut two circles of cardboard 2" (body) and 1½" (head) in diameter and put a hole in the middle that is about ½" in diameter so that it looks like a lifesaver. Cut through the lifesaver on one side so that you can wrap yarn thickly around the entire circle. Cut the loops along the outer edges of the circle and tie an 9" piece of yarn tightly around the center so that it makes a pom-pom. Do this for both sizes of circles and leave the tie ends long. Using the long ends, tie the body to the head. Cut two felt ears, pinch at the bottom and sew to the upper back area of the head. I can make one of these in about 15 minutes using yarn ends (widely available at yard sales) and felt scraps.

✦ **Plastic eggs** that open into halves can be saved and used for years. Fill these with a few jellybeans, pennies, little polished stones, an egg bead on a silk cord, a few chocolate chips or a little toy from your yard sale stash.

✦ **Wooly sheep.** Trace the pattern below onto cardboard and cut it out. Using a permanent marker, color the head black on both sides. Clip two clothespins on indicated marks. Color the "feet" black up to the bottom of the clothespin hinges. You'll need about 40 yards

Ear   Tail

of white yarn. (If you want a chubbier sheep, glue a layer of fiberfill to the body before you begin to wrap yarn.) Wrap yarn from belly to back a few times to secure it, then wrap the whole body, beginning at tail and proceeding to nose. Leave just the black nose sticking out. Wrap figure-eight style around the legs a few times and then just wrap the hinge until it is covered. Tuck in the end of yarn.

Cut ears and tail out of black felt using pattern. Glue one ear to either side of sheep's face and the tail on the back. Tie a ribbon around its neck. This project is easy enough for children to do, and if you're using yard sale yarn, very cheap.

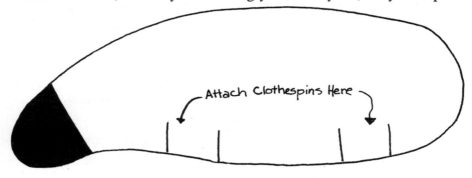

Attach Clothespins Here

✦ **Stuffed animals.** This needn't be a big expense. Yard sales yield a plentitude of new-looking bunnies, that you can put through the a cold water wash and air dry. Tie a new crisp ribbon around its neck and it is hard to tell it from the $10.00 variety. You may have more than enough stuffed bunnies, like we do. This year I opted for smaller country-style muslin bunnies from the hobby store for 99¢.

✦ **Easter bunny finger puppets.** Cut ears and body of felt following the diagram right. Fold a tiny tuck into each ear. Sandwich the ears between the two body pieces and sew them together on the machine or by hand using a whip stitch. Glue on snippets of felt for the face and a piece of cotton ball for the tail. I can make one of these in 15 minutes using felt scraps. Compare this to the time, money and energy it takes to earn the money, take it to the store and spend it.

✦ **Baskets** can be reused from years past. I have a small collection of sturdy baskets and my kids pick one from there to decorate and make ready for the Easter bunny. They decorate it by winding ribbon around the handle and tucking in a few dried flowers here and there.

✦ **Grass.** Plastic basket grass is inexpensive and can be saved from year to year. I personally hate the stuff - it gets in every crack and crevice, messes up the vacuum cleaner, the cat tries to eat it - and I try never to bring it home. Instead, I save crumpled tissue paper in white and pastel colors, fold it accordian fan style, and cut it into strips. Some shredded paper packaging that is used to cushion items for mailing may be used. Save it if you get some with your packages and you hate plastic grass like I do. Another alternative is to save flyers on pastel paper that come your way during the year and give it to someone who has a paper shredder to shred for you.

✦ **Dying eggs.** It is really not necessary to buy egg dyes. Food coloring works great and can be mixed to provide more colors. To two cups of warm water, add a few drops of coloring and 1

teaspoon vinegar. To make them shine, put a few drops of vegetable oil on a paper towel and gently polish the boiled and dyed eggs. If your kids draw on the egg with a light-colored crayon before it is dyed, that portion will remain white. I like basic dyed eggs, but if your kids are clamoring for more decor, try gluing on sequins or glitter, wrapping a ribbon around one or drawing on a face with a permanent marker and gluing on some yarn or Easter grass hair.

✦ **Eggshells with hair.** Take half an eggshell, rinse it out and put a bit of potting soil in the bottom of it. Add some grass seeds or wheat berries. (Wheat berries are wheat kernels that are sold by the pound at a natural foods grocery. You only need one ounce, which costs less than 5¢.) Keep the seeds damp and soon they will sprout into grass. Draw a face on your eggshell with permanent marker. Let the hair be long or give him a crewcut. To display, use a film canister as a stand.

Halloween

Halloween is becoming big business. Remember when, only a few years ago, we were somehow able to live just fine without $25 - $50 costumes for ourselves and our children? We can still live just fine and have great costumes, too, for a few dollars and just a little ingenuity. There are three sources of easy, inexpensive costumes: borrowed, bought second-hand, and ordinary duds transformed for the evening with the aid of a few add-ons.

✦ **Borrowed.** Canvas your friends to see if they have a costume in the size you need. Offer to loan your old ones at the same time. People who have more than one child often have a collection from which to choose.

✦ **Thrift store and yard sale.** I'm in favor of letting children costume themselves in a wide variety of outfits without limiting it to "girl" costumes and "boy" costumes. The reality, however, is that little girls often want to be

some form of princess and little boys often want to be some form of action hero. Since thrift stores are now marking the price of their costume-makings up right before Halloween, I think it is a good strategy to get some components of the costumes as you find them throughout the year. Capes, ball gowns in small sizes and crowns surface frequently in the used clothes market. Store them in your costume box or in the kids' dress-up clothes. Props such as plastic swords and exotic costume jewelry help complete a costume.

If you don't already have them, look to this source for inexpensive leotards and sweatsuits to use with the following costume strategy.

✦ **Add-ons.** This strategy uses some combination of tights, leotards. sweat shirts and pants to which an applique, cape, skirt, sandwich board and/or headdress is added. To a black sweatsuit, you can add white spots and a floppy pair of ears and you have a spotted dog. Take two lengths of ribbon and sew two sizes of felt petals to them (larger for the waist and smaller around the face). Tie on over leotard and tights to transform a child into a flower. Multicolored spots added to a sweatsuit form the foundation for a clown outfit. A wig, facepaint and maybe a neck ruffle finishes it. To apply appliques to garments, either sew in place with basting stitches that can be easily removed or use a product called Stick It Again and Again, which is a kind of glue you put on the back of the applique. (This is available for $1.65 a bottle from Nancy's Notions - see Resources.)

Sandwich boards are two stiff "boards" (like posterboard) that hang down front and back and are tied together at the shoulders. For instance, cut two pumpkin shapes from orange posterboard, draw in the details, glue on a couple of green construction paper leaves and make a wreath of more leaves for the child's hair. Wear a one-color suit in a non-clashing color underneath. This will work with a wide variety of designs and is good for odd requests, like when your son wants to be an apple with a worm sticking out of it, or a scrambled egg.

These ideas are to give you the basic add-on system. Use library books for inspiration and make your own designs. And be sure to check the after-Halloween sales for inexpensive additions to your costume stash and for those gross things that children love year round, like fake spiders and green fingernail polish.

Halloween treats

If you live in a neighborhood with lots of children, bags of candy can be a big Halloween expense. Compare costs based on each portion. If you buy cheaper candy, but compensate by giving out three times as much per kid, you haven't saved anything. Set a price limit per portion, say 10¢. That makes the cost of giving treats to 100 kids $10.00. Knowing your price limit will help when you see possible alternatives. Are Tootsie Roll Pops on sale in bundles of seven for 29¢? Go for it. Are rubber frogs marked down to 15¢ each? That's over your price limit for trick-or-treaters. See a bag of noise makers at a yard sale for 50¢ ? If there are more than 5 in there, take them home to your Halloween box.

Besides candy, I have seen individually wrapped fortune cookies, pennies wrapped in aluminum foil, a few gummy worms tied up in plastic wrap, packs of gum, little erasers, stickers, and glow-in-the-dark pencils. A good source for low-cost treats is the Oriental Trading Company. (See Resources.)

Resources

• *Unplug the Christmas Machine: A Complete Guide to Putting Love and Joy Back Into the Season*, Jo Robinson and Jean Coppock Staeheli, William Morrow, 1991, $9.00.

• *The Children's Year*, Stephanie Cooper, Christine Fynes-Clinton and Marye Rowling, Hawthorn Press, 1982. Crafts for kids and parents by season.

• *The Family Read-Aloud Holiday Treasury*, selected by Alice Low, Little Brown, 1991, $19.95.

• Nancy's Notions. (800)245-5116. Mail order sewing notions and a source of Stick It Again and Again, adhesive backing for fabric appliques that can be removed and re-stuck. $1.65 per bottle.

• Oriental Trading Company, (800)228-2269. Mail-order source of low-cost toys in case amounts. (For example, my last catalog had a case of 36 glow-in-the-dark 8" plastic snakes for $3.25.)

The ancestor of every action is a thought.

Ralph Waldo Emerson

CHEAP LADY! in To Save, Or Not To Save
by Alyssa Reid

Dear Moms (and Dads) Who Want to Come Home,

Are you a parent who wants to spend less time working and more time at home with your children? Do you wonder if you can afford it? A May 1994 *Child* magazine survey of mothers with children below age 13 showed that 48% of mothers who work full-time would prefer cutting back their hours and 30% would prefer to stay home altogether. If you are feeling an urgency now to be with your children while they are young, listen to your heart. A 1990 *Time* magazine poll of 18 - 29 year olds revealed that 63% of them hope to spend more time with their own children than their parents spent with them. I, personally, find it painful to imagine my children growing up to wish they had more time with me.

I want to share with you some information that may change the way you view your job and may open up for you some possibilites. In a study by the U.S. Labor Department, researchers found that *80% of the take home pay* of working mothers was spent on job-related expenses such as transportation, child care, clothes and meals out. In *Your Money or Your Life,* the authors include family meals out due to fatigue, escape entertainment and illness from job stress in the costs of working. I recommend *Your Money or Your Life* to every mother who wishes to come home to help you evaluate the net gain you are receiving for your work. After doing this evaluation, some families have discovered to their astonishment, that having two incomes does not provide them with much of a net gain over having only one job.

One of these families is the Browns (not their real name) of Atlanta, Georgia. "I missed the kids and wanted so much to go to part-time," says Beverly Brown, "but I didn't think we could afford it." Beverly and her husband, Tom, sat down one night after the kids were in bed and totalled up all of Beverly's work-related costs. "I couldn't believe my eyes," exclaims Beverly now. "After costs, I was bringing home $1.75 an hour. I quit the next day."

Beverly used her spunky attitude to figure out how to cut the family's expenses enough to compensate for the small amount she was actually netting in income. Does she feel deprived by their decreased budget? "Are you kidding?" she hoots, rolling her eyes. "It's the best decision I ever made."

That's not all. Mothers at Home (see Resources at the end of this chapter) points out that it is a myth to think that the choice to have a parent at home is only possible in wealthy families. The 1993 Census Bureau Survey reveals that the median income of married couple families with children and a mother at home is $35,876. The median income of married couple families with children in which both parents are employed is $50,621, about $15,000 more. You don't have to be rich to live on one income.

I am not on a soapbox against working moms. I *am* enthusiastic about the freedom I feel and the financial results I've gotten by simply being thrifty. I have felt the pull that millions of women feel when they leave their small children to go to work and I want all women to know that they are not without choices in this situation. Take a look at your choices, use your creative abilities, and you might become one of the many who has found her way home.

With best wishes,

Lisa

Resources

• Mothers at Home is an organization that supports at-home mothers and publishes *Welcome Home*. ($18 per year) Information/Order Line: (800) 783-4MOM.

INDEX

<u>MORE TIPS!</u>   <u>MORE STORIES!</u>   <u>MORE FREEBIES!</u>

Want to keep your enthusiasm high?

**Would you like to have more great ideas, articles
and thrifty inspiration sent to you every month?**

Subscribe to *PurseStrings*! Each newsletter is packed full of articles, ideas from other families, and how-to's for inexpensive toys and entertainment. Join the ranks of families who look to *PurseStrings* for ways to make childraising cheaper and more fun. In *PurseStrings*, you'll find proof that it can be done!

GREAT FUN   LITTLE MONEY

Subscribe by calling toll-free 1-800-795-9587. 12 issues $14.00. (Or send your check to *PurseStrings*, 36 Camino Cielo, Santa Fe, NM 87501.)

PURSESTRINGS
For parents who want to spend less
and enjoy their families more.

Come visit our web page - www.ThriftyLiving.com

ORDER FORM

Phone: Toll free **1-800-795-9487**

E-Mail: to **LisaReid@ThriftyLiving.com**

US Post: **Ferguson-Carol Publishers**
36 Camino Cielo
Santa Fe, NM 87501

YOUR SHIP TO ADDRESS

Name:_____

Street / Apt_____

City_____**State**_____**Zip** _____

Daytime phone: (_____ **) -** _____ **-** _____

Make check or money order payable to
Ferguson-Carol Publishers or use
☐ **Discover**   ☐ **MasterCard**   ☐ **Visa**

Card number:_____

Name on card:_____**Exp.date:**_____

One year subscription to *Pursestrings* newsletter	$ 14.00
Raising Kids With Just A Little Cash books	$ 12.95
Shipping book in US	$ 1.75
NM residents add 5.75% sales tax	
TOTAL ORDER	$_____